TUCK IN

GOOD HEARTY
FOOD ANY TIME

To Ronnie.
For now and for always.

TUCK IN

GOOD HEARTY FOOD ANY TIME

Ross Dobson

MURDOCH BOOKS

SYDNEY · LONDON

my food story

Where would we be without food? Well, yes, we would starve, but aside from the obvious, where would we be without *good* food? Like music, art or even entertainment and fashion, things would get dull very quickly without good food in our lives.

On the most basic level, we need food to sustain us. But it also does so much more; it excites and entices, arouses and seduces, it leads us to explore and discover, and it brings us together.

Like a pop song, a sculpture or even a style of jeans, we all have our own personal take on food. This may be influenced by circumstance, family, friends, culture or just individual taste. And, just like everyone else, I too have my own personal take.

My food story begins in a small country town called Tumbulgum (pronounced Tum-bowl-gum by locals, Tum-bull-gum by everyone else) in northern New South Wales, Australia. There, the brackish Tweed River bends like an elbow. In the crook of the elbow sits the picturesque and bucolic village of Tumbulgum, fenced in by cane fields and the Pacific Highway.

With nowhere to grow, Tumbulgum was the opposite of an urban sprawl and, like every other small town in those days, it was inhabited mostly by white Catholics and white Protestants.

People had names like Dot and Rusty, Joan and Betty, Simms and Twohill. But there was one family in particular that I was drawn to. They had a name like no other. They were the La Rosas. They came from a far-away place called Sicily and had names like Giuseppe, Luigi and Rosetta. And there were more; ten La Rosas in total (Mr and Mrs plus eight kids) lived in a cheddar-yellow Queenslander (a raised wooden house), sandwiched between the local store and the garage.

What the La Rosas did I had never seen done before: they all made food together. Salami was made and hung to dry under the house. Upstairs, silky hand-made pasta was left to dry over broom handles and around the large dinner table; tomato passata was funnelled into recycled brown beer bottles, capped and stored for a rainy day. We had lots of those.

The La Rosas were a loud, colourful and emotional bunch, full of joy and love for good, honest food. And, unwittingly, they did something very important and formative, something that kick-started my obsession with food. As a five-year-old, they gave me my first taste of parmesan cheese. Unbeknown to me at the time, this was my introduction to the fifth taste: umami. Umami is the reason why we love spaghetti bolognese, ramen noodle soup, gravy, soy sauce and Vegemite. And it is very likely that this encounter with parmesan cheese started my lifelong love affair with food.

My dad was a country cop until he, and we, were transferred to Sydney. There we settled in the burgeoning western suburbs where I found myself in food heaven. Our neighbours included Isabel and Jimmy Chung from Hong Kong, the Ibrahims from Cairo (Mrs Ibrahim had the most beautiful name of Mauvette) and the Apokis family from Athens. It was like the United Nations of food and there were no borders. Exotic culinary delights were passed over the fence: dolmades, moussaka, pilaf, won ton soup and the best fried rice ever. I was exposed to truly authentic and mind-blowing flavours. At home, our favourite family meal was roast lamb and veggies and you might be thinking that this couldn't compete with all the other food on offer. But it did. It was good too, and I loved it all.

The food from these cultures, places such as the Mediterranean, Asia and the Middle East, spoon-fed their way into our lives. I discovered ingredients like soy sauce and ginger, parmesan and feta cheese, olive oil and cumin. And it was all prepared by a home cook to be shared. At the end of the day this was all just unpretentious family food—comfort food with lots of flavour.

So here we are. All the recipes in this book reflect my culinary journey. They are all made to share on lots of different occasions in our lives, whether it's a quiet weeknight dinner, a chilled-out barbecue with neighbours or a glittering event with lots of friends. This is food that can be wolfed down and gobbled up. It is food you can really tuck in to.

monday to friday

This chapter's rather prosaic title doesn't really do justice to the exciting recipes that lie within—recipes that pack a punch with minimal effort. We're not talking lengthy lists of ingredients or complicated techniques here. These are quick and easy meals to come home to: hearty soups, comforting pastas and quick curries, or wintry stews that ask for little more than a stir of the pot and just a bit of time.

Planning and a well-stocked pantry are key—and don't be afraid to take a few short cuts. There's nothing wrong with using good-quality ready-made stocks, tinned tomatoes, a packet of soup mix, frozen peas or a barbecued chicken from the supermarket. Combined with fresh vegetables and herbs, meat and seafood, grains, rice and pasta, you'll be able to whip up a meal that will keep the hungry hordes happy and well fed.

Monday to Friday never tasted so good.

This is one of those really easy recipes that will leave you amazed at how tasty the end result is. The star ingredient here is the sambal oelek, so try to find one with very few ingredients: a good sambal is made only with chillies, some vinegar and salt. There are many brands available, though I tend to prefer the Indonesian ones.

chilli sambal and lime leaf drumsticks

2 tablespoons vegetable oil
8 chicken drumsticks, skin on
2 brown onions, cut into wedges
3–4 garlic cloves, chopped
1 tablespoon finely grated ginger
125 g (4½ oz/½ cup) sambal oelek
8 kaffir lime leaves, torn
400 ml (14 fl oz) tin coconut milk
2 tablespoons fish sauce

1 teaspoon light brown sugar
1 Lebanese (short) cucumber, thinly sliced
1 large tomato, sliced
1 red onion, thinly sliced
1 handful coriander (cilantro) sprigs
1 large red chilli, sliced diagonally
2 tablespoons fried Asian shallots

Heat the oil in a large frying pan over medium–high heat and cook the chicken drumsticks for 8–10 minutes, turning often, until the skin is golden.

Add the onions and cook for 4–5 minutes, until the onions have softened, then add the garlic and ginger and cook, stirring constantly, for 1 minute, or until aromatic. Add the sambal oelek, lime leaves, coconut milk, fish sauce, brown sugar and 400 ml (14 fl oz) water. Stir to combine well.

Reduce the heat to medium and simmer for 25 minutes, or until the chicken is cooked through. Cover and set aside for 10 minutes.

To make the salad, combine the cucumber, tomato, onion and coriander in a bowl.

Transfer the drumsticks to a large bowl and garnish with the chilli and shallots. Serve with the cucumber salad and steamed jasmine rice.

NEXT TIME *Use fish instead of the chicken. You will need a firm fish such as snapper fillet, mackerel or ocean trout. Skin on or skin off is fine. The fish won't need to be cooked for as long as the chicken. Pan-fry 4 fish fillets, weighing about 150 g (5½ oz) each, for 4–5 minutes, add the onions and other ingredients, following the recipe above, then simmer over medium heat for 10–15 minutes.*

All the tube-shaped pastas, such as penne, rigatoni, ziti and even fusilli, do like a good baking. Their hollow shapes can be delicious hiding spots for sauce and they make for easy eating. It is common to see baked pasta, or pasta *al forno*, with a tomato-based sauce. Not in this recipe. There is an indulgent group of ingredients here, combining to make a really comforting and delicious meal.

penne rigate with bacon, cauliflower and gorgonzola

300 g (10½ oz) penne rigate
300 g (10½ oz) cauliflower,
    broken into bite-sized pieces
100 g (3½ oz) butter
4 bacon rashers, thinly sliced
3 tablespoons plain (all-purpose)
    flour

¼ teaspoon ground nutmeg
500 ml (17 fl oz/2 cups) milk
150 g (5½ oz) gorgonzola cheese
60 g (2¼ oz/1 cup) fresh
    breadcrumbs

MONDAY TO FRIDAY

Preheat the oven to 180°C (350°F). Bring a large saucepan of cold water to the boil and add a generous pinch of salt. When the water returns to the boil, add the pasta and cook for 7 minutes.

Add the cauliflower to the pan and cook for a further 5 minutes, or until both the pasta and cauliflower are tender. Drain well and then tip the pasta and cauliflower back into the pan. Set aside.

Heat the butter in a saucepan over high heat. Add the bacon and cook for 4–5 minutes, until golden. Add the flour and nutmeg and stir to combine. Gradually add the milk to the pan and cook until the milk thickens. Remove from the heat. Break the cheese into smaller pieces directly into the hot sauce and stir until just combined.

Stir the cheese sauce into the pasta until combined. Transfer to a large baking dish, sprinkle the breadcrumbs over the top, then bake in the oven for 15–20 minutes, until the breadcrumbs are golden and crisp.

NEXT TIME *The inclusion of gorgonzola here has poshed up what is really a basic mac cheese recipe. If this strong-flavoured cheese is not to your liking, replace with a sharp and tasty aged cheddar or gruyère.*

The thing about a quick and comforting soup is that it must be a meal in itself. You don't want to prepare a soup that only serves as a prelude to a main meal. No, that won't do. You want a soup that is tasty and hearty, one that is meant to be enjoyed with some sinful, well-buttered toast or flatbread on the side.

red lentil and sun-dried tomato soup

2 tablespoons olive oil
2 red onions, sliced
2 teaspoons ground cumin
2 garlic cloves, chopped
410 g (14½ oz/2 cups) red lentils
3 tablespoons sun-dried tomato paste
400 g (14 oz) tin crushed tomatoes

1 litre (35 fl oz/4 cups) chicken stock
1 teaspoon chilli flakes
260 g (9¼ oz/1 cup) Greek-style yoghurt
1 large handful coriander (cilantro) leaves
crusty bread, to serve

Heat half the oil in a saucepan over high heat. Add half the onions and stir-fry for 5 minutes, or until golden. Add half the cumin and cook, stirring, for 1 minute, or until dark and aromatic. Tip into a bowl and set aside.

Heat the remaining oil in the saucepan. Add the remaining onion and the garlic and stir-fry for 4–5 minutes, until the onion is soft. Add the lentils and tomato paste and stir to combine. Cook for a couple of minutes, or until the paste darkens slightly.

Add the remaining cumin, the tomatoes, stock, chilli flakes and 500 ml (17 fl oz/2 cups) water. Bring to the boil, stirring to remove any bits stuck to the bottom of the pan. Reduce the heat to medium and cook for a further 20 minutes, or until thick.

Divide among bowls and top with the yoghurt, reserved fried onions and coriander. Serve with crusty bread.

NEXT TIME *For a more substantial meal, add 400 g (14 oz) diced firm white fish fillets to the cooked soup and cook for a further 10 minutes, or until the flesh is opaque and flakes easily when tested with a fork.*

M
O
N
D
A
Y

T
O

F
R
I
D
A
Y

How often do you see a fried rice recipe that calls for several cups of pre-cooked rice? Then you realise how hungry you and your lot are, but you don't have the time to cook the rice, let it cool and then stir-fry it. Here we use an Indian or Middle Eastern technique: the rice is not boiled or steamed beforehand; instead, the grains are stir-fried in a well-seasoned and aromatic oil. Only then is the liquid added and the rice is steamed with just about any ingredient you fancy. Bear in mind the cooking time is brief, so ingredients like chicken and seafood are the go. A barbecued chicken from the supermarket is ideal.

chicken, bacon and egg rice

1/2 barbecued (rotisserie) chicken
2 tablespoons vegetable oil
2 bacon rashers, thinly sliced
2 garlic cloves, chopped
2 tablespoons finely chopped fresh ginger
2 spring onions (scallions), sliced
400 g (14 oz/2 cups) jasmine rice

1 tablespoon light soy sauce
75 g (2$\frac{1}{2}$ oz/$\frac{1}{2}$ cup) frozen peas
750 ml (26 fl oz/3 cups) chicken stock
4 eggs, lightly whisked
1 large handful coriander (cilantro) leaves, finely chopped
sriracha sauce, to serve

Remove the skin from the chicken and thinly slice. Pull the meat off the bones and slice. Discard the carcass.

Heat the oil in a large heavy-based frying pan over high heat. Add the bacon, garlic, ginger and spring onions and stir-fry for 2–3 minutes, until aromatic and the bacon is starting to crisp up. Add the rice and stir until the grains are glossy.

Add the chicken meat and skin, soy sauce and peas and stir to combine, then add the stock. Stir to remove any bits stuck to the bottom of the pan. Once the stock comes to the boil, reduce the heat to low. Cover the pan and cook for 25 minutes, or until the rice is cooked through.

Pour the eggs over the top of the rice, then cover the pan and cook for a further 5 minutes. The eggs will still be runny. Gently stir the mixture to combine the rice with the eggs, then stir in the coriander. Serve with sriracha sauce on the side.

NEXT TIME *If you can source them, use Chinese sausages (lap cheong) instead of bacon. These sausages are available from Asian food stores, but I've also seen them in my local supermarket, air-dried and vacuum-packed. Use two sausages, thinly sliced, and cook them as you would the bacon.*

Apparently, Japanese sumo wrestlers eat this. It's all about the healthy balance of protein and carbohydrates. It's funny how food trends change. If you take a closer look at the ingredients in this, you'll see it is really just meat and three veg—but just a touch more exotic and flavoursome.

sumo pork
and vegetable stew

1 tablespoon vegetable oil
500 g (1 lb 2 oz) pork shoulder, cut into 2 cm (¾ inch) pieces
6 thin slices fresh ginger
2 garlic cloves, coarsely chopped
4 spring onions (scallions), cut into 3–4 cm (1¼–1½ inch) lengths
2 small carrots, chopped

1 large waxy potato, chopped
3 tablespoons red miso paste
60 ml (2 fl oz/¼ cup) light soy sauce
1 teaspoon sugar
75 g (2½ oz/½ cup) frozen peas
1 large handful flat-leaf (Italian) parsley leaves, finely chopped
1 teaspoon sesame oil

Heat the vegetable oil in a heavy-based saucepan over medium–high heat. Add the pork and stir-fry for 4–5 minutes, until the pork is browned all over.

Add the ginger, garlic and spring onions and stir-fry for 1 minute, then add the carrots and potato. Add 1 litre (35 fl oz/4 cups) water to the pan and bring to the boil.

Stir in the miso paste, soy sauce and sugar. Reduce the heat to low and simmer for 1¼ hours, stirring every now and then, until the pork is tender. Stir in the peas and cook for a further 5 minutes.

Serve the stew sprinkled with parsley and drizzled with the sesame oil.

NEXT TIME *Replace the pork with the same quantity of beef chuck. Serve with udon noodles or fresh or dried ramen noodles. If you want something really quick and easy, the noodles in those packets of instant noodle soups would also be a tasty accompaniment.*

I've never really taken much notice of the packets of 'soup mix' in the supermarket. But then I did and I realised how convenient and economical they are. No need to hunt through all the shelves looking for separate packets of lentils, beans and peas. Here they all are, together in one small bag.

scotch broth

1 tablespoon light olive oil
2 large lamb shanks
1 brown onion, chopped
2 celery stalks, diced
1 large carrot, diced
1 bay leaf
200 g (7 oz/1 cup) soup mix
    (cannellini beans; pinto beans;
    yellow, green and red split peas)

100 g (3½ oz/½ cup) basmati
    rice
2 small beef stock cubes,
    crumbled
2 tablespoons finely chopped
    flat-leaf (Italian) parsley,
    plus a small handful of leaves,
    to garnish

Heat the oil in a large saucepan over high heat. Add the lamb shanks and cook for 8–10 minutes, turning the shanks every couple of minutes, until browned evenly all over. Transfer the lamb shanks to a plate.

Add the onion to the pan and stir-fry for about 5 minutes, or until softened and starting to turn golden. Add the celery, carrot and bay leaf and stir-fry for 2–3 minutes, scraping the bottom of the pan to remove any bits that are stuck.

Add the soup mix and stir to combine with the vegetables. Return the lamb to the pan and add the rice, stock cubes and 3 litres (105 fl oz/ 12 cups) water. Bring to the boil, then reduce the heat to low and simmer for 2 hours, turning the lamb and stirring everything every 20 minutes or so. By this time, the lamb meat should be starting to fall off the bone.

Remove the pan from the heat and carefully transfer the lamb shanks to a chopping board. When the lamb is cool enough to handle, remove the meat from the bone and chop into large pieces. Discard the bones and return the meat to the broth. Place the pan over low heat to warm through, then stir in the chopped parsley. Serve garnished with parsley.

 To really beef this up and give this soup a Moroccan slant, add a 400 g (14 oz) tin of rinsed and drained chickpeas and 2 teaspoons ras el hanout to the pan when cooking the veggies.

By any other name, this is pasta *all'amatriciana*, Rome's most iconic pasta dish. The original recipe, from the hillside town of Amatrice, calls for spaghetti, but in Rome it's usually served with bucatini, a thick, hollow spaghetti-like pasta. This messy-to-eat pasta might flick you in the face, but that only adds to the enjoyment. I usually like to add a big handful of spinach leaves to the bowl; it's a sneaky way of eating salad and the flavours work well together too.

pasta with tomato, chilli and pancetta

200 g (7 oz) piece pancetta, cut into 1 cm (1/2 inch) chunks
60 ml (2 fl oz/1/4 cup) olive oil
1 red onion, coarsely chopped
400 g (14 oz) tin crushed tomatoes
1/2 teaspoon chilli flakes

400 g (14 oz) bucatini or perciatelli
100 g (31/2 oz/1 cup) grated pecorino, romano or parmesan cheese
4 large handfuls baby English spinach

Put the pancetta in a large saucepan with the oil and fry over low heat for 15 minutes, or until all the fat has been rendered out and the meat is very crisp. Remove from the pan with a slotted spoon and set aside.

Add the onion to the pan and cook over medium heat for 5 minutes, stirring often. Add the tomatoes, then stir in the chilli flakes. Season with sea salt and freshly ground black pepper. Simmer for 10 minutes, stirring occasionally, until the sauce has thickened slightly.

Meanwhile, bring a large saucepan of cold water to the boil and add a generous pinch of salt. When the water returns to the boil, add the pasta and cook until *al dente*; this will take 9–12 minutes, depending on the brand. Ladle about 125 ml (4 fl oz/½ cup) of pasta water into the pan with the sauce. Drain the pasta.

Add the drained pasta and pancetta to the sauce and stir for 30 seconds, or until well combined and heated through. Remove from the heat and stir in half the cheese.

Put a handful of spinach into each of four serving bowls. Serve the hot pasta over the spinach and scatter the remaining cheese on top.

No pancetta? Simply substitute with bacon or ham. A dollop of fresh ricotta cheese on top of the pasta would be pretty great, too.

I would really encourage you to use Greek oregano (*rigani*) for this recipe. You probably won't find it in your supermarket, so you may need to hunt around for it: try a Greek or Italian deli. It's wonderfully fragrant and sold in bushels or bundles of semi-dried twigs that will keep for ages in an airtight container. The oregano sold in jars sometimes includes 'fillers' such as sumac and dried and crushed olive leaves. These taste nothing like authentic oregano. And besides, it's a cheeky bit of false advertising on the part of the supplier.

roast chicken, lemon and feta soup

2 tablespoons olive oil
4 spring onions (scallions), thinly sliced
4 garlic cloves, chopped
1 tablespoon dried oregano, preferably Greek oregano (rigani)
2 handfuls flat-leaf (Italian) parsley leaves, finely chopped

1/2 barbecued (rotisserie) chicken, skin and meat coarsely chopped
45 g (1½ oz/¼ cup) medium-grain rice
1.5 litres (52 fl oz/6 cups) chicken stock
60 ml (2 fl oz/¼ cup) lemon juice
100 g (3½ oz) feta cheese, crumbled into small pieces

Heat the oil in a saucepan over high heat. Add the spring onions, garlic, oregano and half the parsley. Stir-fry for 2–3 minutes, until aromatic. Add the chicken and rice and stir through for a minute or so.

Pour in the stock, stir to combine and bring to the boil. Reduce the heat to low, then stir in the lemon juice. Simmer for 25–30 minutes, until the rice is cooked and the soup has thickened.

Serve the soup topped with the crumbled feta and remaining parsley, with fresh pita bread on the side.

 Add a 400 g (14 oz) tin of rinsed and drained chickpeas or cannellini beans. Substitute the rice with small pasta.

If you have any left-over roast lamb in the fridge, chop it into small dice and add to the soup instead of the chicken.

How good is the combination of sweet leek and earthy potato ... but isn't there just something missing? Some bacon perhaps? Potato, leek and bacon are often the foundation of a good stew, and I say if they're good enough for a casserole, then they're certainly good enough for a soup. Added to all this goodness is mascarpone and parmesan, which are stirred through at the end.

potato and leek soup ... with bacon

50 g (1¾ oz) butter
4 bacon rashers, thinly sliced
2 large leeks, pale part only, halved lengthways and thinly sliced
2 garlic cloves, chopped
1 litre (35 fl oz/4 cups) chicken stock
1 kg (2 lb 4 oz) potatoes, cut into 2 cm (¾ inch) pieces

240 g (8½ oz/1 cup) mascarpone cheese
25 g (1 oz/¼ cup) grated parmesan cheese
15 g (½ oz/½ cup) finely chopped flat-leaf (Italian) parsley

Heat the butter in a saucepan over medium–high heat. When the butter starts to sizzle, add the bacon and leeks and stir-fry for 4–5 minutes, until the leeks are tender. Add the garlic and cook for 1 minute, taking care not to burn it.

Pour in the stock and bring to the boil. Add the potatoes and cook for about 15 minutes, or until the potatoes are very tender and starting to fall apart.

Reduce the heat to low. Stir in the mascarpone, parmesan and parsley. Season well and serve hot.

Feeling guilty about the mascarpone? It can be substituted with light sour cream. And if pork isn't your thing, omit the bacon.

If you can find some salted cod, this would work perfectly in this recipe. Soak 1 kg (2 lb 4 oz) salted cod in several changes of cold water over a period of 24 hours. Drain and discard the soaking liquid. Boil the cod for 30 minutes, then remove all the skin and bones. Shred the cod flesh and add to the soup with the potatoes.

Blade steak is similar to chuck. In fact, it's from the same part of the animal, although blade often has less fat, which means the cooked result can be drier than if you'd used chuck or gravy beef—but this is not a bad thing. I do like the texture of the blade cut. It holds its form after long cooking times, and it's perfect for use in curries or braises where you want the meat to stay together.

blade steak with bacon, onion and paprika gravy

75 g (2½ oz/½ cup) plain (all-purpose) flour
2 teaspoons sweet paprika
2 teaspoons ground white pepper
2 teaspoons salt
4 blade steaks, bone in, about 200–250 g (7–9 oz) each
50 g (1¾ oz) butter

60 ml (2 fl oz/¼ cup) light olive oil
6 brown onions, thinly sliced
6 bacon rashers, coarsely chopped
375 ml (13 fl oz/1½ cups) chicken stock
1 tablespoon mild mustard
1 small handful flat-leaf (Italian) parsley leaves

Preheat the oven to 180°C (350°F). Combine the flour, paprika, white pepper and salt in a bowl. Press the steaks into the flour to coat evenly all over, then set aside. Reserve the flour mixture to thicken the gravy.

Heat the butter and oil in a large frying pan over medium–high heat. When the butter starts to sizzle, put the steaks in the pan (you may need to cook two at a time) and cook for 4–5 minutes on each side, until the steaks are golden and tinged orange from the paprika. Transfer the steaks to a baking dish or casserole dish.

Pour off all but 2 tablespoons of oil from the pan. Add the onions and bacon and stir-fry for 8–10 minutes, until the onions are soft and golden.

Sprinkle 3 tablespoons of the reserved spiced flour into the pan and stir to combine. Gradually add the stock and stir until the gravy is smooth and thick. Add the mustard and stir until well combined. Pour the gravy over the steaks in the dish, then cover and cook in the oven for 1½ hours, or until tender. Divide the steaks and gravy among four plates and garnish with parsley. Serve with mashed potato.

NEXT TIME *There are a multitude of sides to serve with this. I love it with mash, but rice or couscous would lap up the flavours nicely–or even a pasta like a twisted casarecce.*

So unassuming but so utterly delicious, this takes me back to something we used to simply call 'savoury mince on toast', which was pretty tasty. But this is so much better. If you have a bit more time on your hands, it's worthwhile making your own hummus for the Turkish toast (there's a simple recipe in Next Time); otherwise, good-quality shop-bought hummus is the way to go.

spiced lamb and hummus on toast

SPICED LAMB
2 tablespoons olive oil
1 red onion, thinly sliced
a generous pinch or two of sea salt
300 g (10½ oz) minced (ground) lamb
2 teaspoons ground cumin
2 teaspoons ground coriander
1 teaspoon ground cinnamon
2 teaspoons garam masala
25 g (1 oz/½ cup) chopped coriander (cilantro) leaves

1 large Turkish bread, cut into 4 pieces
250 g (9 oz) good-quality hummus (or see recipe below)
2 tablespoons pine nuts, toasted
1 small handful coriander (cilantro) sprigs
lemon wedges, to serve

To make the spiced lamb, heat the oil in a frying pan over high heat. Add the onion and salt and stir-fry for 2–3 minutes, until the onion is soft.

Add the lamb and use a wooden spoon or spatula to stir the lamb, breaking up any clumps. Cook for 8–10 minutes, stirring often, until the lamb is brown. Add the spices and cook, stirring, for a further 2–3 minutes, until the mixture darkens and becomes aromatic. Remove from the heat and stir in the chopped coriander.

Cut the Turkish breads in half and toast. Spread the hummus over the hot toast, then spoon the spiced lamb on top. Sprinkle with the toasted pine nuts and garnish with coriander sprigs. Serve with lemon wedges.

NEXT TIME *Home-made hummus is one of life's simple pleasures. To make your own hummus, put a 400 g (14 oz) tin of rinsed and drained chickpeas into a food processor with 135 g (4¾ oz/½ cup) tahini, 60 ml (2 fl oz/¼ cup) lemon juice, 2 crushed garlic cloves, 1 teaspoon sea salt and ½ teaspoon ground white pepper. Process to make a chunky paste. Add a couple of tablespoons of cold water to make a creamier hummus.*

The taste of this will depend on the quality of both the sausages and chorizo. Using inexpensive sausages and chorizo will be OK, but the result will be so much better if you hunt down premium pork products. Look for chorizo with lots of spice, especially paprika, as this will flavour and colour the stew.

This is also a great brunch recipe to have up your sleeve. Divide the cooked stew among individual ovenproof dishes and make a small divet in each. Crack an egg into each dish and cook in a hot oven until the egg is cooked to your liking.

sausage, leek and white bean stew

2 tablespoons olive oil
2 leeks, pale part only, thinly sliced
6 pork sausages, each cut into 4 equal pieces
200 g (7 oz) chorizo, thickly sliced
2 tablespoons chopped rosemary
2 x 400 g (14 oz) tins chopped tomatoes
4 tablespoons sun-dried tomato paste
400 g (14 oz) tin white (cannellini) beans,
    rinsed and drained
125 ml (4 fl oz/1/2 cup) red wine

PARMESAN MASH
1 kg (2 lb 4 oz) russet (idaho) or dutch cream
    potatoes, peeled and quartered
100 g (3 1/2 oz) butter
125 ml (4 fl oz/1/2 cup) milk
25 g (1 oz/1/4 cup) finely grated parmesan cheese

Heat the oil in a large saucepan over high heat. Add the leeks and stir-fry for 2–3 minutes, until softened. Add the sausages, chorizo and rosemary and stir-fry for 5–6 minutes, until the sausages are no longer pink.

Add the tomatoes, sun-dried tomato paste, white beans, wine, 250 ml (9 fl oz/1 cup) water and season with salt and freshly ground black pepper. Bring to the boil, stirring to combine the ingredients, then reduce the heat to low and simmer for 30 minutes, or until the sauce has thickened slightly.

To make the parmesan mash, cook the potatoes in a saucepan of salted boiling water for 20–30 minutes, until very tender. Drain and return the potatoes to the hot pan, adding the butter, milk and cheese. Season well with sea salt and mash until smooth. Use a wooden spoon to whip the potatoes for 1 minute, or until creamy. Serve the stew on a bed of parmesan mash.

NEXT TIME *For a tapas-style treat, leave out the mash. Cook the stew for 25 minutes, then add 12 large raw prawns (shrimp), peeled and deveined. Cook for a further 5 minutes, or until the prawns are pink and tender. Serve with crusty bread.*

Use any left-over stew to make pot pies. Put the mixture in 250 ml (9 fl oz/ 1 cup) ovenproof baking dishes. Place a piece of ready-made frozen puff pastry, slightly bigger than the dish, on top of the stew and press around the edges to seal. Prick the top of the pastry with a fork and brush with beaten egg. Bake in a 180°C (350°F) oven for 20 minutes, or until the pastry is golden.

sausage, leek and **white bean stew**   *page 32*

You've seen it too, haven't you? Recipes that claim to be the best—the best ever chocolate cake, the best ever roast chicken or the best hamburger. I sound like a naysayer, but I'm just not convinced. I mean, there's always going to be something better, isn't there? That's why I am more than happy to settle for second best, then there's never the worry of being knocked off the mantle by some new kid on the block. Besides, I know there will always be better chicken curries out there, but this recipe will win the silver medal every time. And that's not a bad thing.

second best ever chicken curry

2 tablespoons vegetable oil
6 chicken drumsticks, skin on
6 boneless chicken thighs, skin on
2 white onions, sliced
2 garlic cloves, chopped
1 tablespoon finely grated fresh ginger
2 teaspoons fennel seeds
2 teaspoons ground cumin
1/2 teaspoon chilli powder
2 tomatoes, chopped
2 carrots, chopped into 2–3 cm (3/4–11/4 inch) cubes
2 potatoes, chopped into 2–3 cm (3/4–11/4 inch) cubes
75 g (21/2 oz/1/2 cup) frozen peas

Heat the oil in a large heavy-based saucepan over medium heat. Working in batches if necessary, add the chicken drumsticks to the pan and cook for 8–10 minutes, turning every couple of minutes until the skin is golden. Remove from the pan.

Add the chicken thighs to the pan and cook for 6–8 minutes, again turning every couple of minutes until the skin is golden. Remove from the pan. The chicken will be undercooked at this stage, but will be cooked through later in the recipe.

Pour off all but 2–3 tablespoons of the cooking fat. Add the onions to the pan and stir-fry for 8–10 minutes, until softened and golden, scraping the bottom of the pan to remove any bits that are stuck. Stir in the garlic, ginger and spices, season well and cook for 1 minute.

Add the tomatoes, carrots, potatoes and 500 ml (17 fl oz/2 cups) water, stirring to remove any bits stuck to the pan.

Return all the chicken and any juices to the pan. Bring to the boil, then reduce the heat to low and simmer for 45 minutes, or until the chicken is almost falling off the bone. Stir in the peas and cook for 5 minutes. Serve with steamed basmati rice.

NEXT TIME *There's no cause for concern if you aren't a 'meat-on-the-bone' sort of person. Replace the chicken drumsticks and thighs with 8 boneless, skinless chicken thigh fillets, cut in half. Pan-fry the chicken thighs for 3 minutes on each side, then return them to the pan with the vegetables and simmer for 25-30 minutes, until cooked through.*

Use any leftovers to make a second best ever chicken pie. Remove any meat from the bones and shred with a fork or roughly chop into small pieces. Put the mixture into an ovenproof dish and use some good-quality shortcrust pastry to make a lid to cover the dish. Seal the pastry around the edge, prick the top with a fork and brush with some milk. Cook in a 180°C (350°F) oven for about 20 minutes, or until the pastry is golden. Serve with mashed potatoes.

I prefer to use a good marinara mix to make a quick and tasty seafood pie. Marinara mix is generally used in tomato-based pasta sauces and is sold in most supermarkets. Some are good, some not so. When looking for a good marinara, look for a mix that looks like fresh seafood, where you can identify all the ingredients: the white fish, the pink fish (like salmon), calamari and prawns (shrimp). Avoid marinara mixes that have parsley or unidentifiable coloured bits thrown in.

fisherman's pie

4 potatoes, peeled and thinly sliced
100 g (3½ oz) butter, diced
1 leek, pale part only, thinly sliced
7 g (¼ oz/¼ cup) chopped flat-leaf (Italian) parsley
3 tablespoons plain (all-purpose) flour

60 ml (2 fl oz/¼ cup) white wine
600 ml (21 fl oz) thin (pouring) cream
750 g (1 lb 10 oz) marinara mixed seafood

Preheat the oven to 180°C (350°F). Cook the potatoes in a saucepan of boiling water for 10 minutes. Drain well and set aside.

Heat half the butter in a saucepan over medium heat. When the butter starts to sizzle, add the leek and parsley and cook, stirring, for about 3 minutes, or until the leek is silky soft. Add the flour, then pour in the wine and stir to make a thick paste. Gradually add the cream and stir until the sauce is smooth, then continue stirring for 2–3 minutes, until the sauce has thickened.

Reduce the heat to low and stir in the mixed seafood. Pour into a large baking dish and arrange the potato slices on top. Scatter the remaining diced butter over the potatoes and season well with sea salt. Cook in the oven for 45 minutes, or until the potatoes are golden and crisp.

 Make a really simple and lovely salmon pie. Replace the marinara mixed seafood with 750 g (1 lb 10 oz) salmon fillet, cut into 2 cm (¾ inch) cubes and cook as per the recipe above. Add a small handful of chopped tarragon along with the parsley. Serve with some steamed greens and old-school dinner rolls.

This tagine makes use of all the fabulous fragrant flavours of Moroccan cookery and the most simple of cooking techniques. Traditionally, the couscous is cooked separately and served alongside the tagine, but there is often so much palaver around cooking couscous that I wanted to make this recipe as easy as possible. The entire meal is cooked in one pot, including the couscous, which is simply stirred through the hot tagine at the end. Its simplicity earns this recipe its title. No offence guys!

bachelor tagine

500 g (1 lb 2 oz) diced lamb leg meat
1 lemon, halved
1/2 teaspoon ground turmeric
1 teaspoon ground ginger
2 teaspoons ground cumin
2 teaspoons paprika
1 teaspoon sea salt

16 green olives
2 handfuls flat-leaf (Italian) parsley leaves, finely chopped
6 small waxy potatoes, washed and halved
190 g (6¾ oz/1 cup) instant couscous
50 g (1¾ oz) butter, diced

Put the diced lamb in a large flameproof casserole dish or heavy-based saucepan. Squeeze the lemon halves over the lamb and then put the lemon in the dish. Add all the spices, salt, olives, half the parsley and 750 ml (26 fl oz/3 cups) water. Stir well to combine.

Place the dish over high heat and bring to the boil, then reduce the heat to low, cover with the lid and simmer for 30 minutes. Add the potatoes, nudging them in between the pieces of lamb. Cover and simmer for a further 45 minutes, or until both the lamb and potatoes are fork tender.

Stir in the couscous, butter and remaining parsley. Cover the dish and remove from the heat. Set aside for 10–15 minutes, until the couscous has absorbed most of the liquid and is cooked. Serve the tagine on the table straight from the cooking dish, with a crisp green salad on the side.

NEXT TIME *Instead of lamb, use the same weight of diced chuck steak, stewing steak or chicken drumsticks (add the chicken at the same time as the potatoes and cook for 30-40 minutes, or until the chicken is cooked through and the potatoes are tender). If meat is not your thing, ditch the lamb and use 4 x 150 g (5½ oz) firm white fish fillets or mackerel cutlets. Just remember, the fish needs far less cooking time than meat. Cook the fish for roughly 15-20 minutes, until the flesh is opaque and flakes easily with a fork.*

The definition of *jalfrezi* is very broad. It has been described as a combination of Indian, Pakistani and Chinese cooking. I get the former two, but I can't really see where the Chinese influence comes in. The meat, generally chicken, is ever so briefly marinated in some curry powder. All the ingredients are then simply thrown into the pot. This is a gentle curry and would be a good one to introduce young children or curry novices to Indian flavours.

easy jalfrezi

6 boneless, skinless chicken thigh
    fillets, each cut into 3-4 pieces
4 tablespoons madras curry powder
40 g (1½ oz) butter
2 red onions, cut into wedges
1 red capsicum (pepper), cut into
    strips

4 garlic cloves, chopped
1 tablespoon grated fresh ginger
400 g (14 oz) tin crushed tomatoes
260 g (9¼ oz/1 cup) plain yoghurt
50 g (1¾ oz/1 cup) chopped
    coriander (cilantro) leaves

Put the chicken in a bowl and add the curry powder. Use your hands to rub the powder all over each piece of chicken. Set aside for 30 minutes to allow the flavours to develop, or cover and refrigerate for 3–6 hours (remove the chicken from the fridge 30 minutes before cooking).

Heat the butter in a large frying pan over medium–high heat. When the butter starts to sizzle, add the onions and stir-fry for 2–3 minutes, until softened. Add the capsicum, garlic and ginger and stir-fry for a further 4–5 minutes, until all the vegetables have softened.

Add the chicken pieces to the pan and stir-fry for 8–10 minutes, until the chicken is cooked evenly all over and the spices are aromatic.

Stir in the tomatoes, scraping the bottom of the pan to remove any bits that are stuck. Add 2 tablespoons of the yoghurt and stir until the yoghurt is fully incorporated into the sauce. Return to the boil, stir in 2 more tablespoons of yoghurt and repeat until all the yoghurt has been used.

Reduce the heat to low and simmer for 10 minutes, or until the sauce has thickened. Stir in the coriander. Serve with steamed basmati rice.

 For an indulgent and rich version of this curry, use 16 large, peeled and deveined raw prawns (shrimp) instead of the chicken. Replace the yoghurt with 250 ml (9 fl oz/1 cup) thick (double/heavy) cream.

This is a good recipe to have up your sleeve. And it's versatile. The thyme, for instance, can be replaced with some rosemary, oregano, marjoram or bay leaf, and you can use white wine or beer if you don't have any red wine lying around. One thing to keep in mind, however, is that it's best to use French-style, or puy, lentils, because they hold their shape nicely with long cooking times. Their Indian cousin, the brown lentil, will cook down to a soft mush—great texture if you're making dhal, but not so good for a slow-cooked recipe such as this.

one-pot lamb shanks
with lentils and pancetta

100 g (3$\frac{1}{2}$ oz/$\frac{1}{2}$ cup) puy lentils or tiny blue-green lentils
200 g (7 oz) piece pancetta, chopped into 1 cm ($\frac{1}{2}$ inch) cubes
250 ml (9 fl oz/1 cup) red wine
500 ml (17 fl oz/2 cups) tomato passata (puréed tomatoes)
6 thyme sprigs
4 lamb shanks, preferably French trimmed
25 g (1 oz/$\frac{1}{4}$ cup) finely grated parmesan cheese

QUICK POLENTA
190 g (6$\frac{3}{4}$ oz/1 cup) fine or instant polenta
500 ml (17 fl oz/2 cups) milk
500 ml (17 fl oz/2 cups) chicken stock

Preheat the oven to 160°C (320°F). Put the lentils, pancetta, wine, passata and thyme sprigs in a large casserole dish. Season with salt and freshly ground black pepper and stir everything to combine.

Lay the lamb shanks, top-to-toe, in the dish. Cover with the lid and cook in the oven for 1 hour. Turn the shanks over, then cover again and cook for a further 1 hour, or until the meat and lentils are tender. Remove the dish from the oven and leave covered while you cook the polenta.

To make the quick polenta, put the polenta in a heatproof bowl. Pour the milk and stock into a saucepan and bring to the boil. Whisk the hot milk mixture into the polenta, cover with plastic wrap and set aside for 10–15 minutes, until the polenta has absorbed the liquid and is cooked.

Divide the polenta among four plates and top with the lamb shanks and lentils. Sprinkle the parmesan over the top.

NEXT TIME *Use ½ cup small pasta or short-grain rice instead of the lentils. Risoni, orzo or the more difficult to pronounce kritharaki will work an absolute treat. They are all similar enough to warrant the same cooking time (10-12 minutes), but keep in mind they require less cooking time than the puy lentil.*

Keep any leftovers and make a pie. Shred the lamb meat and discard the bones. Combine the meat and lentils and transfer to a pie dish. Cover with shortcrust pastry, brush with beaten egg and cook in a 180°C (350°F) oven for 40 minutes.

For this recipe, the rice is not cooked separately, but rather stirred through the hot stew and cooked until tender. I really like this idea, especially when I am pressed for time. The 'carrier' food—the pasta, couscous or rice—is cooked in with the other ingredients rather than cooked in a separate pot and served on the side.

spicy lamb, spinach and basmati rice stew

1 tablespoon vegetable oil
1 brown onion, chopped
2 garlic cloves, finely chopped
1 tablespoon finely grated fresh ginger
2 tablespoons ready-made green masala paste
800 g (1 lb 12 oz) lamb leg meat, cut into 3–4 cm (1¼–1½ inch) cubes
130 g (4½ oz/½ cup) plain yoghurt

125 ml (4 fl oz/½ cup) thin (pouring) cream
250 g (9 oz) frozen spinach
200 g (7 oz/1 cup) basmati rice, rinsed and drained
1 handful coriander (cilantro) leaves, roughly chopped
2 tablespoons lemon juice
toasted flaked almonds, to serve
coriander (cilantro) sprigs, to garnish

Heat the oil in a large heavy-based saucepan over high heat and stir-fry the onion for 4–5 minutes, until golden and soft. Stir in the garlic and ginger and cook for 1–2 minutes, until aromatic. Add the green masala paste and cook for 2–3 minutes, then add the lamb. Cook for a couple of minutes, just until the lamb loses its pink colour.

Add 1 litre (35 fl oz/4 cups) water, stirring to remove any bits stuck to the bottom of the pan, and bring to the boil. Reduce the heat to medium, partially cover the pan and simmer for 45 minutes.

Add the yoghurt, cream and spinach and cook for 15 minutes, stirring often, until the lamb is tender. Stir in the rice, cover the pan and cook over low heat for 10 minutes, or until the rice is just cooked but still firm to the bite.

Remove from the heat and leave covered for 5 minutes, or until the rice is tender. Stir in the chopped coriander and lemon juice. Sprinkle with the toasted almonds and garnish with a few coriander sprigs.

 NEXT TIME *For a simple variation, replace the lamb with the same weight of boneless, skinless chicken thigh fillets, cut into 3–4 cm (1¼–1½ inch) pieces, and cook for the same time as the lamb.*

take it outside

There's nothing easier and more fun than cooking outside. Crank up the heat on the barbecue and let the smoke billow—that delicious piece of rump steak, chicken thigh or pork belly will be transformed to chargrilled perfection.

Take it outside and cook up some skewers—lots of them. The recipes for spicy beef, pork satay or lamb sticks can easily be doubled or tripled to feed a small army. And meat or chicken on the bone allows you to forget the cutlery; use your fingers and you'll be doing Fred Flintstone proud.

This is casual, outdoor eating and it's food made to share—rolled up in silky rice paper, soft tortillas or in a more conventional burger bun.

Celebrate the best things in life: simple food with lots of flavour shared with family and friends.

Before I made this, I watched a few short videos on the traditional American clambake and I was gobsmacked by the amount of effort involved. A large hole is dug in the sand, the hole is lined with rocks, colloquially known as canon balls, and a fire is built on top. When the fire has died down and the rocks are extremely hot, layers of fresh seaweed and canvas sacks soaked in seawater are strewn over the rocks. The food is placed on top and then covered with more seaweed, canvas and rocks to weigh the whole thing down and steam the food. Thankfully, this clambake won't take you hours to prepare and you don't have to be anywhere near a beach. All you need are some oven bags and a barbecue.

oven-bag clambake

1 kg (2 lb 4 oz) cleaned and ready-to-cook clams (vongole)
125 ml (4 fl oz/½ cup) white wine
75 g (2½ oz) butter
1 teaspoon sea salt
½ teaspoon freshly ground black pepper
2 large red chillies, thinly sliced

1 large handful flat-leaf (Italian) parsley leaves, finely chopped
2 spring onions (scallions), thinly sliced
1 chorizo (about 150 g/5½ oz), diced
1 corn cob, cut into 8 small pieces
soft bread rolls, to serve

Preheat the barbecue hotplate to medium. Tip the clams into a large oven bag, then add all the remaining ingredients. Twist the top of the bag and tie into a loose knot. Use the end of a sharp knife to prick a small hole in the top of the bag. Sit the bag on a baking tray and cook on the barbecue for 30–35 minutes, until most of the clams have popped open.

Pour the contents of the oven bag into four large bowls. Serve with soft bread to soak up the delicious juices.

 NEXT TIME *This recipe would work really well with other types of clams or bivalves such as the common mussel. For a bit of an Asian take on the clambake, use 1 kg (2 lb 4 oz) cleaned mussels instead of the clams, a handful of chopped coriander (cilantro) leaves instead of the parsley, and add 2 tablespoons chopped fermented Chinese black beans. Leave out the chorizo in this version.*

I've got a thing for a good burger bun or roll. Not so much a sandwich but a soft bun, filled with some sort of grilled, slow-cooked, braised or pulled meat. Here, the chicken is marinated in an eclectic combination of flavours from all over the place, to make for a very tasty and more-ish chicken burger.

chipotle chicken and provolone brioche burgers

CHIPOTLE CHICKEN
125 ml (4 fl oz /½ cup) chipotle sauce
125 ml (4 fl oz/½ cup) sherry
2 tablespoons dark soy sauce
2 tablespoons lime juice
1 teaspoon garlic powder
1 teaspoon sea salt
6 boneless, skinless chicken thigh fillets

2 tablespoons vegetable oil
2 white onions, sliced into thin rings
8 small brioche buns or soft buns
16 slices provolone cheese

To make the chipotle chicken, put the chipotle sauce, sherry, soy sauce, lime juice, garlic powder and salt in a bowl. Stir to combine well, then add the chicken and toss it around in the bowl to coat in the marinade. Set aside for 30 minutes to marinate, or cover and refrigerate for 3–6 hours (remove the chicken from the fridge 30 minutes before cooking).

Preheat the barbecue hotplate to high and drizzle with 1 tablespoon of the oil. Tip the onions onto the hotplate and use kitchen tongs to evenly spread the onions over the plate, separating the onion rings. Cook for 8–10 minutes, until the onions are soft and starting to turn golden, then stir the onions around on the hotplate and cook for a further 2–3 minutes. Remove from the hotplate and place in a bowl.

Drizzle the remaining oil over the hotplate. Add the chicken and cook for 8 minutes, then turn and cook for a further 7–8 minutes, flattening the chicken by pressing down firmly with a metal spatula. The chicken should be cooked through and dark in colour. Remove and set aside to rest for 10 minutes. Slice the chicken across the grain into 1 cm (½ inch) thick pieces.

Preheat the oven to 160°C (320°F). Cut the brioche buns in half and put the bottom halves on a baking tray. Top each one with some chicken, onion rings and two slices of provolone. Put the brioche lids on top. Cook in the oven for 10 minutes, or until the buns have warmed through and the cheese has just melted. Serve hot.

 It may be stating the obvious, but this would work really well with warm burritos instead of brioche.

And if you have the time or are so inclined, whip up a chimichurri sauce to serve with any version of this. Put 2 large handfuls each of flat-leaf (Italian) parsley and coriander (cilantro) leaves (roughly chop them first) in a food processor with 1 roughly chopped garlic clove, 2 tablespoons chopped, pickled jalapeño, 1 teaspoon dried oregano, 1 teaspoon sea salt and 2 tablespoons olive oil. Process until well combined and then spoon the sauce over the chicken.

chipotle chicken and **provolone brioche burgers** *page 54*

pork belly burgers *page 58*

I do like pork belly when it's cooked to crispy goodness, but I'm also a big fan of unctuous pork belly that results from steaming, slow braising or poaching. The technique here of slow braising the pork belly is a Chinese one and is often referred to as 'red braising'. Cook the pork this way and it can sit in the fridge, ready to be sliced, grilled and added to a burger or sandwich.

pork belly burgers

PORK BELLY
2 garlic cloves, smashed
5 cm (2 inch) piece fresh ginger, peeled and
    thinly sliced
4 spring onions (scallions), halved
125 ml (4 fl oz/½ cup) dark soy sauce
2 star anise
55 g (2 oz/¼ cup) sugar
2 tablespoons salt
800 g (1 lb 12 oz) piece pork belly

CABBAGE AND FENNEL SALAD
¼ Chinese cabbage (wong bok), finely chopped
1 small fennel bulb, trimmed and finely chopped
1 small carrot, coarsely grated
¼ teaspoon caraway seeds
120 g (4¼ oz/½ cup) good-quality mayonnaise
2 spring onions (scallions), thinly sliced diagonally

1 tablespoon vegetable oil
soft bread rolls and butter, to serve
kecap manis, to serve

To cook the pork belly, bring 3 litres (105 fl oz/12 cups) water in a large saucepan to the boil. Add the garlic, ginger, spring onions, soy sauce, star anise, sugar and salt and boil for 10 minutes, to combine the flavours.

Add the pork, moving the pork around in the fragrant liquid so it is fully submerged. Cover the pan and turn off the heat. Leave for 3 hours, then remove the pork from the poaching liquid and refrigerate until ready to cook. (The pork can remain in the liquid after 3 hours, but it must be refrigerated.)

To make the cabbage and fennel salad, combine the salad ingredients in a bowl. Season with sea salt and freshly ground black pepper. Cover and refrigerate until needed. The salad will keep in the fridge for 3–6 hours, but no longer or it will lose its crispness and freshness.

Slice the pork into 5 mm (¼ inch) thick slices. Preheat the barbecue hotplate to high and drizzle with the oil. Cook the pork for 5 minutes on each side, or until aromatic and dark. Transfer to a serving plate to rest for 10 minutes.

Slice the bread rolls in half and butter them. Add a few slices of pork, drizzle with kecap manis and top with the cabbage and fennel salad.

NEXT TIME *Use beef flank instead of pork and cook for the same amount of time. A whole chicken could be braised this way, too. However, if using chicken, there is no need to refrigerate and then cook it further on the barbecue. After braising for 3 hours, simply cool the chicken to room temperature, then shred the flesh and use the meat in a sandwich or salad.*

It seems that you can find at least one Thai restaurant in every suburb these days, although that's hardly surprising because it really is such a dynamic, fresh and delicious cuisine. This chilli jam chicken can be made with such little effort at home, any day of the week.

chilli jam chicken
with grilled greens

6 boneless, skinless chicken
   thigh fillets
2 tablespoons vegetable oil
2 generous pinches of sea salt
300 g (10½ oz) Chinese broccoli
   (gai larn)
lemon wedges, to serve

MARINADE
1 handful coriander (cilantro)
   leaves and stems, chopped
4 garlic cloves, chopped
½ teaspoon ground white pepper
2 tablespoons fish sauce
a large pinch of ground turmeric
60 g (2¼ oz/¼ cup) Thai-style
   chilli jam

Cut several deep incisions into both sides of the chicken thighs and put into a bowl.

To make the marinade, put all the ingredients in a food processor and process to form an aromatic paste. Massage the marinade into the chicken. Set aside for 30 minutes, or cover and refrigerate for 3–6 hours (remove the chicken from the fridge 30 minutes before cooking).

Preheat the barbecue hotplate to medium, drizzle with 1 tablespoon of the oil and sprinkle the salt over the surface of the hotplate. Cook the Chinese broccoli for 2–3 minutes on each side. Put the greens on a serving plate, cover and set aside.

Drizzle the remaining oil over the hotplate. Add the chicken and cook for 8–10 minutes on each side, until the chicken is almost falling apart and the marinade has cooked down to a thick toffee colour. Put the chicken on a chopping board and cut into thick slices.

Serve the chicken on the grilled Chinese broccoli, with lemon wedges on the side and with steamed jasmine rice if desired.

NEXT TIME *Swap the Chinese broccoli for broccolini, broccoli or asparagus. Keep in mind that some vegetables like broccoli are quite hard, so need a longer cooking time, or blanch them in boiling water beforehand.*

This is a very cool way to present a traditional meal and it works really well when taken outside and cooked on a barbecue hotplate. Actually, it is preferable to cook it outside as you can really crank up the barbecue heat without fear of smoking out the house. Feel free to add other ingredients to the salad: capsicum (pepper), tomato, coriander (cilantro) and chopped boiled egg would all be delicious wrapped in the velvety soft rice paper.

curried pork rice paper rolls with vietnamese salad

4 pork scotch fillet steaks, 180-200 g (6¹/2-7 oz) each, no thicker than 1.5 cm (⁵/8 inch)
2 tablespoons madras curry powder
2 tablespoons finely chopped lemongrass (pale parts only)
2 garlic cloves, finely chopped
2 tablespoons vegetable oil
12 large round rice paper sheets, 22 cm (8¹/2 inches) in diameter

HOISIN PEANUT SAUCE
70 g (2¹/2 oz/¹/4 cup) hoisin sauce
2 tablespoons peanut butter
1 tablespoon boiling water
40 g (1¹/2 oz/¹/4 cup) roughly chopped roasted peanuts

VIETNAMESE SALAD
230 g (8 oz/2 cups) bean sprouts
1 carrot, thinly sliced into matchsticks
2 large red chillies, thinly sliced into matchsticks
2 Lebanese (short) cucumbers, sliced into thin strips
1 butter lettuce, washed and leaves separated
10 g (¹/4 oz/¹/2 cup) mint leaves

Put the pork steaks in a bowl with the curry powder, lemongrass, garlic and 1 tablespoon of the oil. Use your hands to combine the ingredients, massaging the pork until coated in the spicy oil. Set aside for 30 minutes, or refrigerate for 6 hours or overnight (remove the pork from the fridge 30 minutes before cooking).

Preheat the barbecue hotplate to high. Drizzle the remaining tablespoon of oil over the hotplate, then cook the pork for 6 minutes on each side. You want the pork to be well done, so it caramelises and is sweet. Remove the pork to a plate and rest for 10 minutes. Slice the pork across the grain into strips no wider than 1 cm (½ inch) and put into a bowl.

To make the hoisin peanut sauce, combine the hoisin sauce, peanut butter and boiling water in a bowl. Transfer to a serving bowl and sprinkle with the peanuts. Set aside.

To prepare the Vietnamese salad, put the bean sprouts, carrot and chillies in a bowl and toss to combine, then transfer to a large platter along with the cucumber strips, lettuce and mint leaves. The salad can be prepared in advance and refrigerated for a couple of hours until needed.

Sit a large bowl of hot water on the table. Briefly dip one sheet of rice paper in the hot water to soften it, but for no more than 10 seconds or the rice paper will be too soft and will break up.

Put a lettuce leaf on the softened rice paper and top with a few slices of pork, some bean sprout and carrot mixture, one or two strips of cucumber and a few mint leaves. Firmly roll the rice paper up into a log shape to enclose the ingredients. Serve with the hoisin peanut sauce.

 Use 4 large boneless, skinless chicken thigh fillets to replace the pork. Cook the chicken for 8-10 minutes on each side.

curried pork rice paper rolls with **vietnamese salad**　*page 62*

This salad is a very popular one in Myanmar, served in just about every cafe and restaurant. Traditionally the salad includes pickled tea leaves, but these are just about impossible to source. They are, however, very easy to make at home. I've included a recipe here if you'd like to add a touch of authenticity, although the salad is still quite tasty without it. The recipe for the beef skewers is an old favourite of mine, with no particular origin.

beef skewers with myanmar salad

BEEF SKEWERS
500 g (1 lb 2 oz) beef fillet, cut into 2–3 cm
　　(3/4–1 1/4 inch) cubes
1 red onion, grated
2 garlic cloves, finely chopped
1 tablespoon grated fresh ginger
2 tablespoons mild curry powder
260 g (9 1/4 oz/1 cup) plain yoghurt

MYANMAR SALAD
250 ml (9 fl oz/1 cup) rice vinegar
2 tablespoons green tea leaves
2 large truss tomatoes
180 g (6 1/2 oz/4 cups) finely shredded Chinese
　　cabbage (wong bok)
3 spring onions (scallions), thinly sliced
　　diagonally
1 large green chilli, thinly sliced
1 tablespoon lime juice
1 tablespoon fish sauce
1 teaspoon sesame oil
40 g (1 1/2 oz/1/4 cup) roughly chopped
　　roasted peanuts
fried Asian shallots, to serve

Soak eight bamboo skewers in cold water for 30 minutes before using.

To make the beef skewers, put the beef cubes in a bowl with some salt and freshly ground black pepper. Add the onion, garlic, ginger, curry powder and yoghurt. Stir to combine and then set aside for 30 minutes, or refrigerate for 3–6 hours (remove the beef from the fridge 30 minutes before cooking).

To make the Myanmar salad, put the rice vinegar, tea leaves and 250 ml (9 fl oz/1 cup) water in a saucepan. Simmer for 30 minutes, then drain. Put the tea leaves in a small bowl.

In a large bowl, combine the tea leaves and all the remaining salad ingredients, except the fried shallots. Toss to combine and then set aside while you cook the beef skewers (this will also allow time for the flavours in the salad to develop).

Preheat the barbecue grill or hotplate to high. Put four or five pieces of meat on each skewer. Add the beef skewers to the hot barbecue and cook for 4 minutes, then turn and cook for a further 3 minutes, or until cooked through. Just before serving, sprinkle some crispy fried shallots over the salad and serve with the beef skewers.

NEXT TIME *Feel like some carbs to serve with the beef skewers and salad? Make a simple spiced potato dish by boiling 4 cups roughly chopped potatoes in boiling water until tender. Tip into a colander and drain well. Heat 2 tablespoons vegetable oil in a large frying pan and stir-fry 1 teaspoon cumin seeds and 1 teaspoon black mustard seeds until sizzling. Add the potatoes to the pan and stir-fry until golden. Add 1 handful of coriander (cilantro) leaves, finely chopped, and the juice of 1/2 lemon. Season to taste and gently toss to combine.*

Za'atar is the general term given to the Middle Eastern blend of dried herbs. The mixture usually includes a combination of sumac, dried thyme, dried marjoram and sesame seeds. Za'atar is not traditionally used as a rub or marinade—although it works well as one—but more as a side condiment to sprinkle over cheese or bread that has been dipped in olive oil. As for the salad, this is so-named for the region in Iran from which it hails. Traditionally, the ingredients would be finely chopped; here they are more chunky.

za'atar lamb
with shirazi salad

SHIRAZI SALAD
2 Lebanese (short) cucumbers,
    cut into large pieces
1 red onion, cut into thin wedges
2 truss tomatoes, cut into wedges
2 tablespoons olive oil
1 tablespoon lime juice
15 g (1/2 oz/1/4 cup) finely chopped
    curly parsley

ZA'ATAR LAMB
2 lamb backstraps or loin fillets,
    about 200 g (7 oz) each
30 g (1 oz/1/4 cup) za'atar
a generous pinch of sea salt
1 tablespoon olive oil
lime wedges, to serve

To make the Shirazi salad, combine all the ingredients in a bowl and set aside. Making the salad a few hours before you need it gives the flavours time to develop.

To make the za'atar lamb, put the lamb on a large plate or tray. Sprinkle the za'atar over the lamb, then roll the lamb around to evenly coat. Set aside for 1 hour or refrigerate for 3–6 hours (leave the lamb uncovered).

Preheat the barbecue hotplate to medium and sprinkle the salt over the surface of the hotplate. Drizzle the oil over the lamb, again rolling the lamb around in the za'atar and oil to coat.

Cook the lamb on the barbecue for 4 minutes, then turn and cook for a further 3 minutes. The lamb will be on the rare side, so cook for a few minutes longer if desired. Remove to a plate and rest for 10 minutes before slicing across the grain into 2 cm (¾ inch) thick pieces. Serve the lamb with the salad, lime wedges and with chargrilled Turkish bread.

 Use beef, turkey or chicken breast fillet, thinly sliced, to replace the lamb.

You can buy labneh—yoghurt that has been strained and rendered thick—but it's actually dead easy to make. All you need is yoghurt, salt and a bit of time. And once you make a batch you will not look back. Smear it on a plate and top with your favourite salad or serve it with grilled meats, especially lamb and beef. I really like the dramatic look of the 'sticks' used here; they are simply bamboo chopsticks, sold in bulk from Asian food stores.

lamb sticks with home-made labneh

LABNEH
1 kg (2 lb 4 oz) plain yoghurt
1 tablespoon salt

LAMB STICKS
500 g (1 lb 2 oz) minced (ground) lamb
100 g (3½ oz) firm feta cheese, coarsely grated
1 white onion, grated
2 garlic cloves, grated
2 teaspoons dried oregano, preferably
    Greek oregano (rigani)
1 teaspoon olive oil
1 tablespoon vegetable oil

1 Lebanese (short) cucumber, diced
2 tomatoes, diced
1 red onion, diced
1 handful mint leaves, thinly sliced
1 lemon, halved

To make the labneh, combine the yoghurt and salt in a bowl. Lay a piece of cheesecloth (muslin) or a clean kitchen cloth over a colander. Pour the yoghurt into the colander and tie the cloth into a tight knot to enclose the yoghurt. Sit the colander in a larger bowl and refrigerate for at least 6 hours or overnight.

Unwrap the cloth and transfer the labneh to a bowl and refrigerate until needed.

Soak eight bamboo chopsticks in cold water for 30 minutes before using. This will prevent them from burning.

To make the lamb sticks, put all the ingredients, except the vegetable oil, in a bowl. Use your hands to squeeze the mixture for a couple of minutes, so the ingredients are really well combined. Throw the mixture onto the side of the bowl or on a clean work surface for 1 minute to tenderise the meat. Divide into eight portions and roughly shape each portion into a sausage shape. Wet your hands and then take one of the lamb portions and press it around the top half of a chopstick (on the thinner end of the stick). Repeat with the remaining lamb and sticks.

Preheat the barbecue hotplate to high and drizzle with the oil. Cook the lamb sticks for 12 minutes, turning often until evenly golden all over. Remove to a plate and allow to rest for 5 minutes.

Combine the cucumber, tomatoes, red onion and mint in a bowl.

Dollop a large spoonful of labneh on each serving plate and use the back of the spoon to smear the labneh over the plate. Top with the lamb sticks and serve with the tomato salad and lemon halves, for squeezing over the lamb. Any left-over labneh can be stored in a sealed container in the fridge for up to 3 days.

NEXT TIME *Harissa is the traditional chilli paste used in Moroccan cooking and is lovely served with lamb. There are many versions, but to make this easy version, simply soak 100 g (3½ oz) large dried red chillies in boiling water for 1 hour, then drain well. Snip the stem ends off the chillies and squeeze out most of the seeds (it's fine if a few remain). Put the chillies in a food processor with 2 garlic cloves, 2 teaspoons cumin seeds, 1 teaspoon sea salt and 125 ml (4 fl oz/½ cup) olive oil. Process for 1–2 minutes to make a thick red paste. Transfer to a container and store in the fridge for 2–3 weeks.*

lamb sticks with **home-made labneh** *page 70*

For this to be a real success, try to get your hands on some free-range pork chops. To be honest, I have a hard time telling the difference in taste between non-free-range and free-range chicken; however, I think free-range pork is in a league of its own and well worth the extra expense—not to mention the ethical considerations.

red-braised pork chops
with warm gingery slaw

4 pork chops
1 tablespoon vegetable oil

RED BRAISING LIQUID
250 ml (9 fl oz/1 cup) dark soy sauce
250 ml (9 fl oz/1 cup) light soy sauce
60 g (2¼ oz/¼ cup, firmly packed) light brown
    sugar
3 star anise
2 cinnamon sticks
3 spring onions (scallions), green part chopped

GINGERY SLAW
2 tablespoons vegetable oil
1 tablespoon sesame oil
½ Chinese cabbage (wong bok), shredded
½ head radicchio, shredded
1 large tomato, cut into wedges
3 spring onions (scallions), white part thinly
    sliced diagonally
2 large red chillies, thinly sliced
2 tablespoons finely grated fresh ginger
2 garlic cloves, grated
1 tablespoon light soy sauce
1 tablespoon rice vinegar
1 large handful coriander (cilantro) leaves
    and stems, roughly chopped

To prepare the red braising liquid, put all the braising ingredients in a large saucepan with 2 litres (70 fl oz/8 cups) water and bring to the boil for 5 minutes. Remove from the heat and set aside to cool.

Add the pork chops to the braising liquid, moving them around so they are fully submerged in the liquid. Set aside for 3 hours or refrigerate for up to 24 hours (remove the pork from the fridge 30 minutes before cooking).

Preheat the barbecue hotplate to medium–high and drizzle with the oil. (You could also use a large heavy-based frying pan to cook the pork.) Cook the pork for 5 minutes, then turn the pork over and cook for a further 5 minutes. Remove to a plate and cover with foil while you prepare the slaw, leaving the barbecue on medium–high.

To make the gingery slaw, pour the vegetable and sesame oils into a large roasting tin and put the tin on the hotplate. When the oil is just starting to smoke, add the cabbage, radicchio, tomato, spring onion, chillies, ginger and garlic and stir-fry in the tin for 1–2 minutes, until the vegetables have just wilted. Remove from the heat, add the soy sauce and vinegar and stir to combine. Stir in the coriander.

Serve the pork chops with the gingery slaw and pour over the cooking juices from the pork.

 Use lamb cutlets instead of the pork chops. You will probably need 3 lamb cutlets per person.

The success of this dish depends entirely on the cut of meat you use. You're looking for high-quality grilling steak, but this shouldn't cost a bomb—that's why I prefer rump steak over other cuts of beef. The other important part of this recipe is the spicy sauce; I could drink this stuff. Not really, but you know what I mean. What makes the sauce really special is the combination of fresh and dried chillies. Fresh chilli brings a 'raw' hotness to the sauce while the dried chillies impart a smoky depth of flavour.

crying tiger

4 x 180 g (6½ oz) pieces rump steak
1 tablespoon light soy sauce
2 tablespoons uncooked glutinous (sticky) rice
1 tablespoon vegetable oil

SPICY DIPPING SAUCE
60 ml (2 fl oz/¼ cup) fish sauce
2 tablespoons sugar
2 tablespoons tamarind concentrate

juice of 1-2 limes
1½ tablespoons best-quality Thai chilli flakes
1 tablespoon finely chopped small red chillies
1 tablespoon thinly sliced red onion or Asian shallots
1 tablespoon finely chopped coriander (cilantro) leaves
1 tablespoon finely chopped mint

Put the steaks and soy sauce in a bowl. Toss the meat around to coat in the soy sauce. Set aside for 1 hour.

Put the rice in a small frying pan. Cook over medium heat, shaking the pan, until the rice is golden brown and fragrant. Tip into a bowl and cool, then put in a spice mill or grind with a pestle and mortar to a powder.

To make the spicy dipping sauce, combine all the ingredients in a bowl, stirring to dissolve the sugar. This can be done up to a day in advance, to allow the flavours to develop.

Preheat the barbecue hotplate to high and add the oil. When smoking hot, cook the rump steaks for 3 minutes on each side for medium-rare. Remove to a board and rest for 5 minutes. Slice the beef across the grain and serve sprinkled with the roasted rice powder, with the dipping sauce in a bowl on the side. I like to eat this with some lightly chargrilled Asian greens—such as bok choy (pak choy) or choy sum, halved lengthways and cooked on a lightly oiled barbecue—and some steamed jasmine rice.

 Use pork scotch fillet instead of the beef. Serve the pork with steamed rice or tossed with some stir-fried egg noodles.

This is a fusion of Vietnamese and Mexican cooking. *Cha ca* is a Vietnamese recipe using turmeric and dill to give both colour and flavour to the grilled fish—and it's delicious. The fish is served in the most quintessentially Mexican way: with avocado and soft tortillas.

vietnamese fish tacos with avocado and pickled onions

CHA CA FISH
4 skinless flathead fillets, halved lengthways
125 ml (4 fl oz/½ cup) tinned coconut cream
2 tablespoons lime juice
1 teaspoon ground turmeric
1 tablespoon grated fresh ginger
2 tablespoons finely chopped dill
½ teaspoon sea salt

PICKLED ONION
2 tablespoons rice vinegar
1 tablespoon sugar
1 teaspoon salt
½ teaspoon chilli flakes
1 large red onion, thinly sliced

8 soft wheat tortillas
1 tablespoon vegetable oil
80 g (2¾ oz/2 cups) good-quality mixed baby salad leaves
2 avocados, ripe but firm, thinly sliced
lemon wedges, to serve (optional)

To make the *cha ca* fish, put the flathead in a metal or glass bowl (anything else will be stained by the turmeric) with the coconut cream, lime juice, turmeric, ginger, dill and salt. Set aside at room temperature for about 30 minutes.

To make the pickled onion, combine the vinegar, sugar, salt and chilli flakes in a bowl. Add the onion and use your fingers to separate the onion slices. Set aside for 5–10 minutes, until the onion has softened and turned a vibrant pink colour.

Wrap the tortillas loosely in foil, folding the edges over to seal. Preheat the barbecue hotplate to high. Put the wrapped tortillas on the hotplate for 2 minutes, then turn and heat for a further 2 minutes. Remove from the hotplate and leave wrapped in the foil to keep warm.

Drizzle the oil over the hotplate. Add the fish pieces and cook for about 4 minutes on each side, or until the fish flakes easily when tested with a fork. Remove the fish to a tray to cool a little, then roughly break the fish into smaller pieces.

Fill the warm tortillas with some mixed salad leaves, sliced avocado and fish, and top with the pickled onions. If you like, serve with lemon wedges to squeeze over the fish.

 Use ocean trout fillets or large, raw prawns (shrimp) instead of the flathead.

If you like, serve this with some simple coriander rice. Stir 100 g (3½ oz/ 2 cups) roughly chopped coriander (cilantro) leaves, 1 tablespoon fish sauce and 1 teaspoon freshly ground black pepper into 750 g (1 lb 10 oz/ 4 cups) cooked jasmine rice (drained well and hot).

vietnamese fish tacos with **avocado** and **pickled onions**   *page 78*

This satay is so fragrant and delicious, and has a lovely golden colour from the turmeric. The inclusion of condensed milk in the satay sauce seems odd, but it is actually used in cooking all over Southeast Asia in both food and hot and cold beverages.

pork satay

500 g (1 lb 2 oz) pork fillet, thinly sliced across the grain
1 tablespoon vegetable oil

MARINADE
1 red onion, chopped
4 garlic cloves, chopped
1 lemongrass stem, pale part only, chopped
1/2 teaspoon ground turmeric
1 teaspoon ground cumin
1 teaspoon ground coriander

1 tablespoon fish sauce
1 tablespoon sugar

SATAY SAUCE
2 tablespoons ready-made Thai prawn and chilli paste
400 ml (14 fl oz) tin coconut cream
3 tablespoons condensed milk
1 tablespoon fish sauce
2 tablespoons tamarind concentrate
70 g (2 1/2 oz/1/2 cup) ground raw peanuts

To make the marinade, put all the ingredients in a food processor. Add 2–3 tablespoons boiling water and process to make a chunky and fibrous paste. Tip the paste over the pork and use your hands to massage the marinade into the pork. Cover and refrigerate for 6 hours or overnight (remove the pork from the fridge 30 minutes before cooking).

To make the satay sauce, put all the ingredients, except the peanuts, in a food processor and process to make a thick paste. Pour into a saucepan and bring to the boil. Stir in the peanuts and cook for 2–3 minutes until thickened. Set aside to cool. The satay sauce can be made several hours in advance.

Soak 12 bamboo skewers in cold water for 30 minutes before using. Thread three or four pieces of pork onto each skewer, pushing the pork towards one end of the skewer. Preheat the barbecue hotplate to medium–high and brush with the oil. Cook the pork skewers for 8 minutes, turning every couple of minutes, until cooked through.

Arrange the pork skewers on a platter with the satay sauce in a bowl, to dip the meat into. Serve with steamed jasmine rice.

 NEXT TIME *This is a very versatile recipe. Try king prawns (jumbo shrimp), chicken, lamb or beef, even firm tofu or paneer.*

Pork scotch fillet has just a nice amount of fat to keep the meat tender when cooked, and the fat also gives the meat a little extra flavour. It's versatile too: the whole piece can be sliced into steaks to be grilled or barbecued, cubed for a stir-fry, or thinly sliced and threaded onto bamboo skewers for a satay.

barbecued pork
with chilli and lime

800 g (1 lb 12 oz) pork scotch fillet, in one piece
1 tablespoon vegetable oil
1 handful coriander (cilantro) leaves and stems, chopped
2 Lebanese (short) cucumbers, thinly sliced diagonally

MARINADE
8 large dried red chillies
4–6 coriander (cilantro) roots, cleaned and roughly chopped

4 garlic cloves, roughly chopped
½ teaspoon ground white pepper
125 ml (4 fl oz/½ cup) Thai oyster sauce

CHILLI LIME DRESSING
2 tablespoons fish sauce
60 ml (2 fl oz/¼ cup) lime juice
½ teaspoon chilli powder
4 red Asian shallots, thinly sliced
15 g (½ oz/¼ cup) finely chopped coriander (cilantro) leaves

Cut the pork lengthways into several thick steaks, about 1 cm (½ inch) thick, and put into a bowl.

To make the marinade, soak the dried chillies in boiling water for 10 minutes. Drain and put the chillies in a food processor with the coriander roots, garlic, white pepper and oyster sauce. Process to form a thick, glossy paste. Rub the marinade into the pork. Cover and refrigerate for 6 hours or overnight (remove the pork from the fridge 30 minutes before cooking).

To make the chilli lime dressing, combine all the ingredients in a bowl.

Preheat the barbecue hotplate to medium and drizzle with the oil. Cook the pork for 8 minutes on each side, or until dark golden in colour. Remove to a plate and set aside to rest for 10 minutes before slicing it across the grain into 1 cm (½ inch) thick slices. Put the pork in a bowl, pour over the dressing, then add the coriander and cucumber. Toss until just combined.

Use beef scotch fillet or lamb backstraps or loin fillets to replace the pork. Fish cutlets, such as mackerel or salmon, are best here, as they will hold their own with the dominant flavours in the sauce.

The defining ingredient here is the Sri Lankan curry powder, which you'll need to buy from a specialty store. This is unique because it is sold as a pre-roasted product so it has a much more intense aroma than other curry powders and is very dark in colour. My local Asian food store supplies lots of brands of Sri Lankan curry powder. Ask if you can smell before you buy. If you feel like it's not your thing, use a mild curry powder instead.

sri lankan chicken with spiced red rice

6 large boneless, skinless chicken thigh fillets
1 handful coriander (cilantro) leaves
1 tablespoon vegetable oil

MARINADE
260 g (9¼ oz/1 cup) plain yoghurt
1 tablespoon tomato paste (concentrated purée)
3 tablespoons Sri Lankan curry powder
1 small brown onion, coarsely chopped
4 garlic cloves, chopped
5 cm (2 inch) piece fresh ginger, peeled and chopped
1 handful coriander (cilantro) stems, coarsely chopped

SPICED RED RICE
300 g (10½ oz/1½ cups) red basmati rice
2 tablespoons coconut oil
1 tablespoon cumin seeds
1 teaspoon black mustard seeds
3 green cardamom pods, crushed with the back of a spoon
8-12 curry leaves
60 ml (2 fl oz/¼ cup) lime juice

Cut the chicken thighs in half and put them in a large bowl with the coriander leaves. Set aside.

To make the marinade, put the yoghurt, tomato paste, curry powder, onion, garlic, ginger and some salt and freshly ground black pepper in a food processor. Add the chopped coriander stems to the marinade and process to make a flecked green paste. Tip the paste into the bowl with the chicken and toss the chicken to coat in the marinade. Set aside for 30 minutes or refrigerate for 3–6 hours (remove the chicken from the fridge 30 minutes before cooking).

To make the spiced red rice, cook the rice in a saucepan of lightly salted boiling water for 10 minutes. Drain, shaking the colander to remove the excess water. Tip the rice into a bowl and set aside.

Heat the coconut oil in a saucepan over high heat. Add the cumin and mustard seeds, cardamom pods and curry leaves to the oil. When the spices start to sizzle and pop in the oil, add the rice and stir to combine. Stir in the lime juice and season with salt and pepper. Cover to keep warm and set aside while you cook the chicken.

Preheat the barbecue hotplate to high. Drizzle the oil over the hotplate, then add the chicken and spread it out over the plate. Spoon any remaining marinade over the chicken. Reduce the heat to medium and cook for 8 minutes. Turn the chicken over and cook for a further 8 minutes, or until the chicken is very dark and cooked through.

Serve the chicken with the spiced red rice and your favourite salad.

NEXT TIME *It's easy enough to make your own roasted curry powder. Put your favourite shop-bought or home-made curry powder in a clean, dry frying pan. Cook over medium heat, shaking the pan until the spices just start to smoke and are aromatic. Remove from the heat, tip into a bowl and allow to cool before storing in a container.*

sri lankan chicken with **spiced red rice** *page 84*

I love a good rissole. It must have something to do with home cooking and comfort eating as a child. The inclusion of spices such as cumin, turmeric and cinnamon, and the home-made tomato sauce make these much more interesting than most other rissole recipes, and the recipe for the tahini crème will become a go-to.

cumin lamb rissoles with tahini crème

LAMB RISSOLES
500 g (1 lb 2 oz) minced (ground) lamb
1 large potato, grated
1 large brown onion, grated
2 tablespoons ground cumin
1 teaspoon ground turmeric
1 teaspoon ground cinnamon
2 teaspoons sea salt
1 tablespoon vegetable oil

TAHINI CRÈME
270 g (9$^{1/2}$ oz/1 cup) tahini
1 teaspoon sea salt
$^{1/2}$ teaspoon ground white pepper
1 tablespoon lemon juice

TOMATO SAUCE
1 tablespoon olive oil
400 g (14 oz) tin chopped tomatoes
1 large handful flat-leaf (Italian) parsley,
    roughly chopped

To make the lamb rissoles, put all the rissole ingredients, except the oil, in a bowl. Use your hands to squeeze the mixture for a couple of minutes, until all the ingredients are well combined. Wet your hands and form the mixture into balls about the size of a golf ball. Set aside for 30 minutes.

To make the tahini crème, put the tahini, salt, pepper and lemon juice in a food processor and whiz for just a few seconds until thickened. With the food processor running, slowly pour in 125 ml (4 fl oz/½ cup) cold water and process until the mixture has a creamy consistency, like putty-coloured custard.

To make the tomato sauce, put the oil and tomatoes in a small saucepan and stir over high heat until the mixture boils. Season to taste and stir in the parsley. Cover to keep warm and set aside.

To cook the rissoles, preheat the barbecue hotplate to high and drizzle with the oil. Put the rissoles on the hotplate and press down with a metal spatula to flatten. Cook for 8 minutes on each side, or until cooked through. Remove to a plate and set aside to rest for 10 minutes.

To serve, spread the tahini crème over a large serving plate. Arrange the meatballs in a single layer on the crème and pour the tomato sauce over the top.

NEXT TIME *Replace the minced (ground) lamb with minced beef. Add some nuts, such as pine nuts or slivered almonds, to the rissole mixture before rolling the meat into balls.*

fine food from far flung places

The exciting flavours of the world have never been closer to us, either literally at our doorstep in the supermarket or at our fingertips on the internet. Nowadays, it's pretty easy to get our hands on just about any ingredient and bring different cuisines and flavours into our homes.

Southeast Asian and Middle Eastern ingredients have made their way onto our shopping lists and into our pantries. Couscous, ras el hanout, labneh, fish sauce and tamarind sit comfortably alongside old-school ingredients; kaffir lime, galangal and Thai basil sit beside mint and parsley in the fridge.

In this chapter, you'll find recipes for favourites such as moussaka and spanakopita along with exotic recipes for a piquant Khmer duck salad, a delicious green curry of pork and a hearty beef kefta.

Let the journey begin.

There's a magic to Portuguese cooking—even the most basic dish can make you feel like a talented cook. The same can be said of much of South American cookery. Rarely do these cuisines call for complicated techniques or a lengthy list of ingredients, and yet the results are truly senstional. This is an honest way to cook, using a few simple key ingredients and will unlock the door to big, hearty flavours and comfort food like no other.

feijoada assado
(pork and bean stew)

2 pork hocks
2 teaspoons sea salt
1 tablespoon olive oil
3 white onions, chopped
2 carrots, chopped
3 garlic cloves, chopped
1 bay leaf

125 ml (4 fl oz/^{1}/$_2$ cup) white wine
500 g (1 lb 2 oz) ripe tomatoes, chopped
1 teaspoon smoked paprika
300 g (10^1/$_2$ oz/1^1/$_2$ cups) dried white (cannellini) beans

Preheat the oven to 150°C (300°F). Wash the pork hocks and pat dry with paper towel. Rub 1 teaspoon of the salt over the pork.

Heat the oil in a heavy-based flameproof casserole dish over high heat. Sit the pork hocks in the dish, side by side, and cook for 10–12 minutes, turning the pork often, until the skin is well browned. Remove the pork from the dish and set aside.

Add the onions, carrots, garlic and bay leaf to the dish, stirring to combine and remove any bits stuck to the bottom of the dish. Cover and cook for 5 minutes, or until the vegetables have softened. Pour in the wine and stir again to remove any stuck-on bits, and cook for 1 minute. Stir in the tomatoes, paprika, white beans and remaining teaspoon of salt.

Return the pork hocks to the dish and add 1.5 litres (52 fl oz/6 cups) water. Nuzzle the pork hocks in the dish, so the white beans are evenly spread around them. Bring everything to the boil, then cover with a tight-fitting lid, transfer to the oven and cook for 3 hours. Remove from the oven and leave to rest, covered, for 30 minutes. Serve with steamed rice.

NEXT TIME *If chilli is your thing, add 1 teaspoon chilli powder, cayenne pepper or chilli flakes when you add the paprika to the dish. To freshen things up a little, roughly chop a few handfuls of coriander (cilantro) leaves and stir them into the stew just before serving.*

You may be familiar with fattoush, the Mediterranean summer salad of fresh vegetables tossed with toasted, left-over bread. Well, fatteh is similar; it comes from the same region but isn't as widely known. Basically, stale flatbread is toasted and given a new and crispy lease of life. It is broken into smaller pieces and loosely layered with the other ingredients. This method comes from the Arabic word *fatta*, which means 'to break into pieces'. Fatteh is often eaten as a breakfast dish, but I think it would be great as a meal on a hot summer's night.

fatteh
(pita bread, chicken and yoghurt salad)

1 x 1.6 kg (3 lb 8 oz) chicken
1 lemon, halved
2 tablespoons olive oil
1 teaspoon sea salt
6 thyme sprigs
3 pita breads, torn into small pieces
1 white onion, thinly sliced
2 tablespoons white wine vinegar
2 garlic cloves, crushed
260 g (9¼ oz/1 cup) Greek-style yoghurt
400 g (14 oz) tin chickpeas, rinsed and
    drained well
10 g (¼ oz/¼ cup) finely chopped flat-leaf
    (Italian) parsley
15 g (½ oz/¼ cup) finely chopped coriander
    (cilantro) leaves
15 g (½ oz/¼ cup) finely chopped mint
2 tablespoons pine nuts, toasted
1 small handful coriander (cilantro) sprigs,
    to serve
1 small handful mint leaves, to serve
lemon wedges, to serve

Preheat the oven to 180°C (350°F). Wash the chicken with cold water and pat dry with paper towel. Squeeze the lemon halves over the chicken, rubbing the lemon juice all over the skin. Put the lemon halves in the cavity. Transfer to a roasting tin. Rub the oil over the chicken skin, sprinkle with the salt and scatter the thyme sprigs over the top.

Roast the chicken in the oven for 1½ hours, or until the skin is golden and crisp. Remove and set aside to cool. When the chicken is cool enough to handle, remove the skin and roughly chop. Remove the flesh and use your hands to shred the meat into 1 cm (½ inch) wide pieces. Put the chicken meat and skin into a large bowl. Refrigerate until needed.

Put the torn pita bread on a baking tray and cook in the oven for about 8 minutes, or until golden and crisp. Randomly arrange the crisp pita on a large serving plate. Combine the onion and vinegar in a small bowl and set aside.

Remove the chicken from the fridge. Add the garlic, yoghurt, chickpeas and chopped herbs to the bowl of chicken. Use your hands to combine everything, then put the chicken and yoghurt mixture on top of the pita.

Drain off any excess vinegar from the onion, then scatter the pickled onion and the pine nuts over the chicken. Garnish with coriander sprigs and mint leaves and serve with wedges of lemon for squeezing over.

NEXT TIME *For a vegetarian version of this recipe, replace the chicken with 300 g (10½ oz) soft feta cheese, roughly broken into bite-sized pieces, and 4 roughly chopped vine-ripened tomatoes.*

If you are short on time, use a barbecued (rotisserie) chicken rather than roasting your own. Alternatively, prepare the chicken the day before.

fatteh (pita bread, chicken and yoghurt salad) *page 96*

khmer roast duck salad *page 100*

While Peking duck enjoys widespread popularity in China, as you move south into other Asian countries, roast duck is more often used in lighter dishes such as salads. Here, the techniques and flavourings used in cooking ducks—many of them taken from Chinese cookery—are incorporated with fresh salad ingredients like tomato, cabbage, snake (yard-long) beans and lots of fresh herbs, with fish sauce and lime juice as a base for a tangy and piquant dressing to complement the duck. These fresh and unique flavours are so typical of the cuisines of Thailand, Cambodia, Laos and Vietnam.

khmer roast duck salad

ROAST DUCK
1 duck, about 2 kg (4 lb 8 oz)
2 garlic cloves, sliced
5 cm (2 inch) piece fresh ginger, thinly sliced
60 ml (2 fl oz/¼ cup) dark soy sauce
½ teaspoon Chinese five-spice
1 teaspoon sea salt

SALAD
½ Chinese cabbage (wong bok), finely shredded
110 g (3¾ oz/1 cup) bean sprouts
2 large red chillies, thinly sliced
1 Lebanese (short) cucumber, finely shredded
1 carrot, finely shredded
2 spring onions (scallions), thinly sliced diagonally
2 snake (yard-long) beans, very thinly sliced
50 g (1¾ oz/1 cup) roughly chopped mint
50 g (1¾ oz/1 cup) roughly chopped Vietnamese mint
30 g (1 oz/1 cup) Thai basil leaves
70 g (2½ oz/½ cup) roasted peanuts, roughly chopped

SALAD DRESSING
2 teaspoons sugar
2 tablespoons fish sauce
60 ml (2 fl oz/¼ cup) lime juice

To roast the duck, rinse the duck with cold water and pat dry with paper towel. Put the garlic and ginger in the cavity of the duck, then transfer to a roasting tin. Combine the soy sauce, five-spice and salt in a small bowl. Rub the soy mixture all over the skin of the duck. Set aside for 1 hour.

Preheat the oven to 160°C (320°F). Place the duck in the oven and cook for 1½ hours, then increase the oven temperature to 220°C (425°F) and cook for a further 10-15 minutes, until the skin starts to darken.

Remove the duck from the oven and leave in the roasting tin for 1 hour, to allow time for the flavours to develop. Pour off 60 ml (2 fl oz/¼ cup) of the pan juices into a cup and set aside.

Remove the duck skin and thinly slice it. Finely shred the meat. Put the skin and meat in a bowl and pour over the reserved juices.

While the duck is cooking, make the salad. Combine all the salad ingredients, except the peanuts, in a large bowl and refrigerate until needed. (I prefer the salad ingredients to be chilled before adding the duck and the salad dressing, as it adds to the flavour experience.)

To make the salad dressing, combine the ingredients in a small bowl, stirring to dissolve the sugar.

To serve, add the duck to the chilled salad and then use your hands to gently combine. Add the dressing and gently toss to combine. Serve on a platter with the peanuts scattered over the top.

NEXT TIME *All the flavours in this dish would work just as well with lamb. Marinate 2 lamb backstraps or loin fillets in 2 tablespoons dark soy sauce and ½ teaspoon Chinese five-spice for 1 hour at room temperature. Sprinkle with sea salt, then cook the lamb on a hot barbecue until done to your liking. Thinly slice the lamb across the grain and combine with the salad.*

Variations of this wonderfully homely style dish can be found pretty much all over Central and South America. The tangy, herbaceous mixture of coriander, garlic and chilli can be used like chimichurri—delicious with grilled fish, chicken, lamb and beef or as a dipping sauce for empanadas.

arroz con pollo
(rice with chicken)

1 large handful coriander (cilantro) leaves and stems
3 garlic cloves, roughly chopped
4 large red chillies, chopped
1 teaspoon sea salt
2 tablespoons olive oil
4 chicken drumsticks, skin on
4 chicken thigh cutlets, skin on
1 red onion, sliced
1 green capsicum (pepper), thinly sliced
75 g (2½ oz/½ cup) frozen or fresh peas
400 g (14 oz/2 cups) long-grain rice
750 ml (26 fl oz/3 cups) chicken stock
2 tablespoons lime juice

Put the coriander, garlic, chillies and salt in a food processor and process to a coarse paste. Set aside.

Heat the oil in a large, wide heavy-based saucepan over medium–high heat. Add the chicken drumsticks and cook for 4–5 minutes, turning often, until golden. Remove from the pan. Allow a minute or two for the pan to reheat, then add the chicken thighs and cook for 8–10 minutes, turning often, until golden. Remove from the pan.

Pour off all but 2 tablespoons of oil from the pan. Add the onion and capsicum and stir-fry for a couple of minutes, until soft. Stir in the coriander paste and the peas and cook for 2–3 minutes, until the paste is aromatic, then add the rice and stir until well combined.

Return the chicken pieces to the pan and pour in the stock. Bring to the boil, then reduce the heat to low, cover and cook for 20 minutes. Remove the pan from the heat and set aside for 10 minutes, with the lid on. Add the lime juice and stir until well combined. Serve hot.

NEXT TIME *Make this with fish instead of chicken, using vegetable or fish stock instead of the chicken stock. There's no need to brown the fish off first. Instead, add 750 g (1 lb 10 oz) firm white fish fillets, cut into large bite-sized pieces, to the pan with the stock and proceed as per the recipe.*

You can easily make this soup at home and create something very close to an authentic *tom yum goong*. The quantity of chillies may seem alarming but you don't actually eat them. They simply float around in the soup, making you feel cautious of them yet imparting their essential flavour. Pick them out after cooking if you prefer or feel free to halve the quantity of chillies at the start if too much heat isn't your thing. The soup is typically served with rice, to offset some of the heat. Keep this in mind whenever you eat food that is laden with chilli—it's not water that provides the antidote to chilli heat, but the steamed rice that helps to cool the mouth.

tom yum goong
(thai hot and sour prawn soup)

400 g (14 oz/2 cups) jasmine rice

4–6 coriander (cilantro) roots, cleaned and roughly chopped

1 large handful coriander (cilantro) leaves and stems, chopped

4 lemongrass stems, pale and light green parts only, chopped

8–10 cm (3¼–4 inch) piece galangal, peeled and thinly sliced

6 kaffir lime leaves, roughly torn

3 litres (105 fl oz/12 cups) chicken stock

4 spring onions (scallions), cut diagonally into 3–4 cm (1¼–1½ inch) lengths

2 tomatoes, cut into thin wedges

1 teaspoon sugar

1 teaspoon sea salt

16 bird's eye chillies, halved lengthways

16 large, raw prawns (shrimp), peeled and deveined, with tails intact

300 g (10½ oz) oyster mushrooms, roughly chopped

2 tablespoons Thai chilli jam

60 g (2¼ oz/¼ cup) tamarind concentrate

60 ml (2 fl oz/¼ cup) fish sauce

60 ml (2 fl oz/¼ cup) lime juice

1 small handful kaffir lime leaves, extra (optional)

To make the accompanying rice, wash the rice in a colander or sieve until the water runs clear. Drain well and transfer the rice to a saucepan with 750 ml (26 fl oz/3 cups) cold water. Bring to the boil and cook for a couple of minutes, or until bubbling holes start to appear over the surface of the rice. Reduce the heat to low, then cover the pan and cook for 20 minutes. Remove from the heat and leave covered while you cook the soup.

Put the coriander roots, coriander leaves and stems, lemongrass, galangal and torn lime leaves in a food processor and pulse a few times, no more. You just want to smash the ingredients, not purée them. Alternatively, put the ingredients in a mortar and pound with a pestle to make a fibrous-looking mixture. Set aside.

Put the stock in a saucepan and bring to the boil. Add the spring onions, tomatoes, sugar and salt and stir to combine. Cook for a couple of minutes, until the tomatoes start to break down. Stir in the lemongrass mixture and the chillies and cook for a further 2–3 minutes, stirring so all the ingredients are well combined.

Add the prawns, mushrooms and chilli jam and cook for 4–5 minutes, until the prawns are pink and just cooked through.

Stir in the tamarind, fish sauce, lime juice and extra lime leaves, if using, then remove the pan from the heat. Cover and set aside for 5–10 minutes. This will allow enough time for the flavours to really develop. Serve the soup with the rice.

NEXT TIME *Feeling like an extravagant seafood soup? Cut the meat from a lobster tail into large bite-sized pieces and add to the soup as you would the prawns (shrimp); gently simmer until the lobster is pink and tender. Scallops and crab would be great here, too.*

tom yum goong (thai hot and sour prawn soup) *page 104*

It may seem unusual to see a baguette served with this beef stew, but considering the French colonial influence in Vietnam, it isn't so odd. Vietnamese baguettes, known as *banh mi*, make a very tasty alternative to rice, which is what you would expect to eat with a Vietnamese beef stew. I have also seen *banh mi* served with chicken curry and chilli crab.

bo kho
(vietnamese beef stew)

MARINADE
4–6 coriander (cilantro) roots
1 large handful coriander (cilantro) stems
    and leaves
1 lemongrass stem, pale part only, roughly
    chopped
4 garlic cloves, roughly chopped
1/2 teaspoon ground white pepper
1 tablespoon oyster sauce
1 tablespoon fish sauce

500 g (1 lb 2 oz) chuck steak, cut into 2–3 cm
    (3/4–1 1/4 inch) pieces
2 tablespoons vegetable oil
2 white onions, cut into wedges
2 star anise
1 cinnamon stick
2 carrots, chopped
250 ml (9 fl oz/1 cup) chicken stock
1 tablespoon oyster sauce
1 tablespoon fish sauce
Vietnamese baguettes or crusty bread,
    to serve

To make the marinade, clean the coriander roots thoroughly, then roughly chop them. Roughly chop the coriander stems, then put the chopped roots and stems in a food processor. Chop the coriander leaves separately and set aside (to later use as garnish). Add the lemongrass, garlic, white pepper, oyster sauce and fish sauce to the food processor and process to form a thick paste. If you don't have a food processor, the ingredients can be finely chopped by hand and combined.

Put the beef pieces in a bowl. Rub the marinade all over the beef and set aside for 30 minutes. This can be done in advance and then covered and refrigerated for up to 24 hours (remove the beef from the fridge 30 minutes before cooking).

Heat the oil in a heavy-based saucepan or flameproof casserole dish over high heat. Add the onions and stir-fry for 2–3 minutes, until softened. Add the marinated beef and stir-fry for a couple of minutes, until the beef changes colour.

Add the star anise, cinnamon stick, carrots, stock, oyster sauce and fish sauce. Bring to the boil, stirring to remove any bits stuck to the bottom of the pan. Reduce the heat to low and partially cover the pan with a lid. Cook for 1½ hours, or until the beef is tender and the aromatic flavours have filled the room. Sprinkle the reserved coriander leaves over the beef and serve with baguettes.

NEXT TIME *Serve the stew with some Vietnamese tomato rice instead of the baguettes. Stir-fry 370 g (13 oz/2 cups) cooked jasmine rice in a wok with 1 tablespoon vegetable oil, 2 finely chopped garlic cloves, ½ teaspoon ground white pepper and 1 tablespoon tomato paste (concentrated purée). Cook until hot and well combined.*

Replace the beef with 6 chicken thighs, skin on and on the bone. Marinate the chicken and then follow the recipe above, noting that the chicken will only need 45 minutes to cook after being browned.

This word, *khoresh*, flows off the tongue. It is so much more romantic and evocative than 'stew' or 'casserole', which is pretty much what it is. *Khoresh* is the staple of many Persian meals and, just like any comforting, home-cooked stew or casserole, simply eating it is enough to make you feel loved and safe.

lamb khoresh (persian stew)

125 ml (4 fl oz/$\frac{1}{2}$ cup) olive oil
2 brown onions, chopped
3 tablespoons tomato paste (concentrated purée)
1 kg (2 lb 4 oz) boneless lamb shoulder, cut into bite-sized pieces
$\frac{1}{2}$ teaspoon ground turmeric
$\frac{1}{2}$ teaspoon ground cinnamon

220 g (7$\frac{3}{4}$ oz/1 cup) yellow split peas
4–5 dried limes (limoo amani)
500 ml (17 fl oz/2 cups) chicken stock
1 teaspoon rosewater
1 kg (2 lb 4 oz) all-purpose potatoes such as desiree, chopped into 2.5 cm (1 inch) pieces

Heat 2 tablespoons of the oil in a large heavy-based saucepan over medium heat. Add the onions and stir-fry for 4–5 minutes, until soft. Stir in the tomato paste and cook for a couple of minutes, until the paste darkens in colour.

Add the lamb and cook for 8–10 minutes, stirring often so the lamb is evenly cooked all over. Stir in the turmeric and cinnamon and cook for 1 minute.

Add the split peas and dried limes, then pour in the stock. Stir to remove any bits stuck to the bottom of the pan. Bring to the boil, then reduce the heat to low and simmer, covered, for 1$\frac{1}{4}$ hours, or until the lamb is very tender and the split peas are cooked but not mushy. Check on the liquid during the cooking time—if it looks too dry, add a cup of water. Stir in the rosewater. Remove from the heat and set aside, covered, while you cook the potatoes.

Put the remaining oil and the potatoes in a frying pan and cook over medium heat for 15 minutes, stirring occasionally. The potatoes will slowly cook in the oil and then, as the temperature of the oil increases, they will turn crispy and golden. Serve the stew with the fried potatoes.

NEXT TIME *Just about anything can be used in this stew. Replace the lamb with beef. Pumpkin (winter squash) and potato (skin on for both is fine) would be great in this, as would okra. For a vegan version, add your favourite veggies and replace the chicken stock with vegetable stock.*

This traditional noodle dish is popular in Northern China. Noodles, in general, dominate the cuisine of the north while rice is grown in the warmer south. Many Chinese dishes aren't always easy for the home cook to make, although this spicy dish is an exception: you don't need a wok, tons of oil or a deep-fryer—just an everyday frying pan.

zha jiang mian
(beijing spicy pork noodles)

1 Lebanese (short) cucumber
3 spring onions (scallions)
2 teaspoons sichuan peppercorns
2 tablespoons vegetable oil
2 garlic cloves, finely chopped
5 cm (2 inch) piece fresh ginger, peeled and grated

500 g (1 lb 2 oz) minced (ground) pork
3 tablespoons chilli bean paste
2 tablespoons dark soy sauce
2 tablespoons light soy sauce
60 ml (2 fl oz/¼ cup) chicken stock
½ teaspoon sugar
100 g (3½ oz) fresh udon noodles

Cut the ends off the cucumber and roughly peel. Cut into matchsticks and refrigerate until needed. Finely chop two of the spring onions and set aside. Finely shred the remaining spring onion to use as garnish.

Put the sichuan peppercorns in a small frying pan and cook over high heat until they begin to smoke. Tip the hot peppercorns into a small bowl and cool. When cool, put into a mortar and pound with the pestle, or grind into a powder using a spice mill.

Heat the oil in a frying pan over high heat. Add the garlic, ginger and chopped spring onions and stir-fry for a few seconds, until fragrant. Add the pork and half the ground sichuan pepper and stir-fry for 4–5 minutes, until browned, using a wooden spoon to break up any clumps of pork. Stir in the chilli bean paste, dark and light soy sauces, stock and sugar. Cook until the liquid has almost evaporated. Set aside.

Cook the noodles in a pan of boiling water for 2–3 minutes, until slippery and tender. Drain and put into a large serving bowl. Pour the pork sauce over the noodles and top with the chilled cucumber and shredded spring onion. Serve with the remaining sichuan pepper, to sprinkle over the top.

NEXT TIME *Replace the pork with the same quantity of minced (ground) chicken–the cooking time will be the same. And, if you like, swap the udon noodles for a packet of two-minute noodles.*

On a recent trip to Northern India with friends, we made it our personal foodie mission to try the biryani wherever we went. Not just because we loved it so much, but also because it became an interesting experiment in how one dish can have many subtle variations. Closer to home, wherever that is for you, this popular rice dish is bound to be on the menu at your local Indian restaurant. But for all this, I had never made biryani myself. So, I sat down at my desk and surrounded myself with books, a computer and lots of notes. My aim was to deconstruct the biryani. It has many levels, so this was easy to do. I then wanted to remove any extraneous steps and reconstruct the recipe so it would be one I would cook again. Here it is.

chicken biryani

400 g (14 oz/2 cups) basmati rice
6 chicken thigh cutlets, skin on
3 tablespoons ghee, or 2 tablespoons vegetable
    oil plus 1 tablespoon butter
2 brown onions, thinly sliced
125 g (4½ oz/1 cup) slivered almonds
125 g (4½ oz/⅔ cup) sultanas (golden raisins)
a generous pinch of saffron threads
60 ml (2 fl oz/¼ cup) warm milk
2 tablespoons rosewater
1 handful coriander (cilantro) leaves,
    roughly chopped
lemon wedges, to serve (optional)

MARINADE
260 g (9¼ oz/1 cup) plain yoghurt
1 teaspoon ground turmeric
2 teaspoons ground cumin
1 teaspoon sweet paprika
1 teaspoon chilli powder
1 teaspoon garam masala
a generous pinch of ground nutmeg
1 cinnamon stick, roughly broken
6 cardamom pods, crushed
1 teaspoon sea salt

Soak the rice in cold water for 10 minutes, then drain and rinse. Cook the rice in a saucepan of boiling water for 5 minutes, then tip into a colander and leave to drain. The rice needs to be undercooked at this stage.

Wash the chicken pieces and pat dry with paper towel. Make several cuts across the chicken, going through the skin. Put the chicken pieces in a bowl or dish.

To make the marinade, combine the yoghurt, spices and salt in a small bowl. Pour the marinade over the chicken and use your hands to rub the marinade all over the chicken pieces. Set aside while you prepare the other elements of the biryani.

Heat the ghee in a heavy-based flameproof casserole dish or large saucepan over medium heat. When the ghee has melted and is sizzling, add the onions and cook for 8–10 minutes, stirring every now and then until golden. Stir in the almonds and sultanas. When the almonds are brown, use a slotted spoon to remove the onion mixture to a plate.

Combine the saffron threads, warm milk and rosewater in a small bowl and set aside.

Add three pieces of chicken to the casserole dish, placing them skin side down, and cook for 8–10 minutes. Turn the chicken over and cook for a further 5 minutes. Remove to a plate and repeat with the remaining three pieces of chicken, then remove them from the dish.

Drain all but a thin layer of oil from the dish and reduce the heat to low. Scatter one-third of the rice over the bottom of the dish, then pour over one-third of the milk mixture. Lay three pieces of chicken on the rice and scatter half of the onion mixture over the top. Repeat with another layer of rice, milk mixture, chicken and onion mixture, finishing with the remaining rice and milk.

Cover the dish and cook over low heat for 30 minutes. Remove from the heat and set aside, covered, for 15–20 minutes, to allow the flavours to develop and the chicken to rest. Before serving, stir in the coriander. If you like, serve with a few lemon wedges for squeezing over.

 Substitute the chicken with 500 g (1 lb 2 oz) diced lamb leg.

chicken biryani *page 114*

This stew cum soup is traditionally eaten during Ramadan. The list of ingredients is fairly extensive, but it is well worth the effort. This makes for a delicious and hearty meal and is just mildly spiced so it can be enjoyed by young and old.

harira (moroccan lamb soup)

500 g (1 lb 2 oz) lamb leg or shoulder meat, cut into bite-sized pieces
1 teaspoon ground turmeric
2 teaspoons paprika
2 teaspoons ground cinnamon
2 teaspoons ground ginger
1 brown onion, chopped
2 garlic cloves, chopped
2 tablespoons olive oil
2 celery stalks, chopped
1 small carrot, chopped
2 bay leaves

1 litre (35 fl oz/4 cups) chicken stock or water
400 g (14 oz) tin chopped tomatoes
400 g (14 oz) tin chickpeas, rinsed and drained
110 g (3¾ oz/½ cup) brown lentils, rinsed
1 handful flat-leaf (Italian) parsley leaves, chopped
1 handful coriander (cilantro) leaves, chopped
lemon wedges, to serve

Put the lamb in a bowl. Add the turmeric, paprika, cinnamon, ginger, onion and garlic and use your hands to massage the fragrant spices into the lamb. Set aside.

Heat the oil in a large heavy-based saucepan or flameproof casserole dish over high heat. Add the celery, carrot and bay leaves and stir-fry for 2–3 minutes, until the vegetables are softened. Add the lamb and scrape any of the spices from the bowl into the pan as well. Stir-fry the lamb for 8–10 minutes, until the lamb is brown and the spices are fragrant.

Add the stock and tomatoes and stir to combine and remove any bits stuck to the bottom of the pan, then add the chickpeas, lentils, parsley and coriander. Bring to the boil, then reduce the heat to low. Cover the pan and simmer for 1½ hours, or until the lamb is very tender. Serve the lamb with lemon wedges to squeeze over.

NEXT TIME *Left-over soup makes a great pie filling. Transfer the left-over harira to an ovenproof dish. Top with puff pastry, brush with butter and sprinkle over some sesame seeds. Cook in a 180°C (350°F) oven until the pastry is golden and the filling is hot.*

This intriguing dish is often said to be one of South Africa's national dishes. *Bobotie* combines flavours that at first seem ... well ... just wrong. But, when cooked, this initial feeling of trepidation gives way to a feeling that you are eating something wonderfully old-fashioned and delicious.

bobotie
(south african savoury mince bake)

2 slices white bread
500 ml (17 fl oz/2 cups) milk
1 tablespoon light olive oil
2 brown onions, thinly sliced
2 garlic cloves, chopped
1 kg (2 lb 4 oz) minced (ground) beef

4 tablespoons madras curry powder
85 g (3 oz/$\frac{1}{2}$ cup) raisins
2 tablespoons fruit chutney
2 tablespoons apricot jam
8 bay leaves
2 eggs

Preheat the oven to 180°C (350°F). Put the bread in a bowl with the milk and soak for a couple of minutes. Remove the bread and squeeze out the excess milk. Set the soaked bread aside and reserve the milk.

Heat the oil in a large saucepan over high heat. Add the onions and stir-fry for 5 minutes, or until softened. Stir in the garlic and cook for 1 minute. Add the beef and stir-fry for 8–10 minutes, until browned, using a wooden spoon to break up the mince into small pieces.

Stir in the curry powder, raisins, chutney, jam and 4 bay leaves and cook for 2–3 minutes, until the spices in the curry powder are aromatic. Add the soaked bread, stir to combine, and season well with sea salt and freshly ground black pepper. Transfer the mixture to a large baking dish.

Measure 250 ml (9 fl oz/1 cup) of the reserved milk into a bowl. Beat the eggs into the milk and pour over the beef mixture. Arrange the remaining bay leaves over the top. Bake in the oven for 45 minutes, or until the custard mixture has set to a golden brown. Serve with sliced banana tossed in shredded coconut.

NEXT TIME *Minced (ground) beef is traditionally used for this recipe, but I think pork would be right at home with all the sweet and spicy flavours going on.*

I have seen this recipe in many incarnations, many of which have been woefully beaten around to produce a rather bland baked concoction. This should not be the case. Greek cuisine uses lots of aromatic spices, herbs and vegetables to produce exciting and fresh-tasting food. This classic dish, with its layers of eggplant (aubergine), potato and beef, topped with a creamy béchamel, also happens to be very hearty and comforting.

moussaka
(lamb, eggplant and potato pie)

60 ml (2 fl oz/¼ cup) olive oil
1 large eggplant (aubergine), cut into 2–3 cm
    (¾–1¼ inch) cubes
2 large potatoes, peeled and thickly sliced
1 tablespoon dried oregano, preferably
    Greek oregano (rigani)
1 brown onion, chopped
2 garlic cloves, chopped
750 g (1 lb 10 oz) minced (ground) lamb
½ teaspoon ground allspice
4 cloves
1 cinnamon stick
1 tablespoon plain (all-purpose) flour
400 g (14 oz) tin crushed tomatoes
2 tablespoons tomato paste (concentrated
    purée)

WHITE SAUCE
100 g (3½ oz) butter
75 g (2½ oz/½ cup) plain (all-purpose) flour
750 ml (26 fl oz/3 cups) milk
½ teaspoon salt
½ teaspoon ground cinnamon
100 g (3½ oz) finely grated graviera
    or pecorino cheese
2 egg yolks, lightly whisked

Preheat the oven to 180°C (350°F). Pour 2 tablespoons of the oil into a large baking dish. Add the eggplant, potatoes and oregano and season with sea salt. Cook in the oven for 30 minutes, or until the vegetables have softened slightly and are just starting to turn golden. Remove from the oven and set aside in the dish.

Heat the remaining oil in a large frying pan over high heat. Add the onion and stir-fry for about 5 minutes, or until soft. Add the garlic and cook for 1 minute. Add the lamb and stir with a wooden spoon to break up any large clumps of meat. Cook for 10–15 minutes, stirring every now and then, until the meat is brown and quite dry.

Stir in the allspice, cloves and cinnamon stick and cook for 1 minute, until fragrant. Add the flour and cook, stirring, for 1 minute.

Add the tomatoes and tomato paste to the pan and stir to combine. Season with salt and freshly ground black pepper. You now want to bring the liquid to the boil and, as the flour cooks in the boiling liquid, it will thicken it. Pour the thickened meat and tomato mixture over the par-cooked vegetables in the baking dish and set aside.

To make the white sauce, heat the butter in a saucepan over medium heat until the butter has melted and starts to sizzle. Remove the pan from the heat and add the flour, stirring to make a smooth paste. Return to the heat and stir for 1 minute. Slowly add the milk, stirring to combine. Continue until all the milk has been incorporated, then cook until the mixture starts to simmer and thicken. Add the salt, cinnamon and cheese and stir to combine. Remove the pan from the heat and stir in the egg yolks. Pour the white sauce over the lamb mixture and cook in the oven for 40 minutes, or until the white sauce topping is golden.

Remove the moussaka from the oven and allow to rest for 15–20 minutes. Cut into squares and serve with a green salad.

NEXT TIME *Turkey is not traditionally used in moussaka, but it's a good alternative to the lamb. Minced (ground) turkey is lean and would go really well with the cinnamon and allspice.*

moussaka (lamb, eggplant and potato pie) *page 122*

This is an amazing pie. It's sexy looking and tastes delicious. The pie is baked upside down and then flipped over after baking to reveal a very professional-looking and perfectly golden pastry sprinkled with sesame seeds.

spanakopita
(spinach filo pie)

FILLING
1 tablespoon olive oil
500 g (1 lb 2 oz) baby English spinach,
    roughly chopped
1 teaspoon sea salt
6 eggs, lightly whisked
130 g (4$^{1/2}$ oz/$^{1/2}$ cup) Greek-style yoghurt
125 ml (4 fl oz/$^{1/2}$ cup) thin (pouring) cream
150 g (5$^{1/2}$ oz) feta cheese, crumbled
15 g ($^{1/2}$ oz/$^{1/4}$ cup) chopped dill
7 g ($^{1/4}$ oz/$^{1/4}$ cup) chopped flat-leaf (Italian)
    parsley
3 spring onions (scallions), sliced

125 g (4$^{1/2}$ oz) butter, melted
1 tablespoon sesame seeds
10 sheets filo pastry

To make the filling, heat the oil in a large frying pan over high heat. Add the spinach and sir-fry for 2–3 minutes, until tender. Remove from the heat, stir in the salt and set aside to cool. Transfer the cooled spinach to a bowl and add the remaining filling ingredients. Stir to combine.

Preheat the oven to 180°C (350°F). Lightly brush some of the melted butter over the base and sides of a 23 cm (9 inch) square or round cake tin. Sprinkle the sesame seeds over the base.

Lay a sheet of filo pastry on the work surface and brush with melted butter. Lay another sheet on top and brush with butter. Lay these two sheets into the cake tin, gently pressing into the tin, allowing some pastry to overhang the sides. Repeat with two more sheets of pastry and lay these in the opposite direction to the first two sheets. Repeat twice more. Brush the remaining two pastry sheets with butter and set aside.

Carefully pour the spinach filling into the tin. Fold the filo over to enclose the filling. Put the reserved pastry on top and tuck it in, then brush the top with butter. Cook in the oven for 40 minutes, or until the pastry is crisp and golden. Remove and set aside to cool for 10–15 minutes.

Invert the pie onto a clean chopping board or large plate. Slice into thick wedges to serve.

NEXT TIME *Substitute the baby English spinach for 1 kg (2 lb 4 oz) silverbeet (Swiss chard), trimming off the tough stalks. Or, for a completely different take on this recipe, cut 2 large eggplants (aubergines) into bite-sized pieces, place on an oiled baking tray and cook in a 180°C (350°F) oven until golden. Use this cooked eggplant instead of the spinach.*

spanakopita (spinach filo pie) *page 126*

kota me hilopites (braised chicken with pasta) *page 130*

It was only recently that I had the pleasure of eating a chicken and pasta dish at a Greek restaurant. Until then, I had never seen chicken and pasta used in the same dish and, to be honest, I never imagined it could be anything special. How wrong I was. The chicken was slow-braised with lashings of olive oil, garlic, tomatoes, red wine and oregano, and had a wonderful depth of flavour that's achieved by cooking chicken on the bone.

The combination of chicken and pasta is very typical of the cuisines of southern Italy and Greece, with each region using its own unique pasta. I've used hilopites here, a Greek pasta about the size of a small postage stamp—Italian quadretti pasta could also be used. Don't worry if you can't find either: simply use fresh fettuccine, cut into small squares.

kota me hilopites
(braised chicken with pasta)

3 chicken Marylands (leg quarters)
1 tablespoon dried oregano, preferably
    Greek oregano (rigani)
125 ml (4 fl oz/$\frac{1}{2}$ cup) olive oil
1 brown onion, grated
4 garlic cloves, chopped
1 cinnamon stick
400 g (14 oz) tin crushed tomatoes
375 ml (13 fl oz/$1\frac{1}{2}$ cups) chicken stock
2 handfuls flat-leaf (Italian) parsley leaves,
    roughly chopped
95 g ($3\frac{1}{4}$ oz/$\frac{1}{2}$ cup) hilopites pasta
100 g ($3\frac{1}{2}$ oz) graviera or pecorino cheese,
    grated

Preheat the oven to 160°C (320°F). Wash the chicken pieces and dry well. Sprinkle the oregano over the chicken.

Heat the oil in a large flameproof casserole dish over medium–high heat. Add the chicken in batches and brown on all sides. Remove and set aside.

Add the onion and garlic to the dish and cook for 4–5 minutes until golden, then add the cinnamon stick, tomatoes, stock, chicken pieces and half of the parsley. Season well and allow the mixture to come to a rapid boil. Cover with a tight-fitting lid or foil, transfer to the oven and cook for 1½ hours, or until the meat is starting to separate from the bone.

Add the pasta to the sauce and stir to combine, then return the dish to the oven and cook for a further 10 minutes. Remove and set aside to rest for 10 minutes. By now, the pasta should have absorbed most of the sauce and be cooked through and the chicken should be falling off the bone.

Divide the chicken and pasta among four plates. Sprinkle with the remaining parsley and the grated cheese.

NEXT TIME *Instead of the chicken Marylands, use 6 chicken thigh fillets or a combination of thigh cutlets and drumsticks, preferably skin on and on the bone. And to take it up a notch, add about 80 g (2¾ oz/½ cup) small kalamata olives.*

All meatball recipes, the world over, have their own special touch: this Moroccan version uses breadcrumbs. I spent some time in Marrakesh, cooking in a riad kitchen, and it was there I saw day-old *kesra*, the delicious, locally made bread, used in the kefta mix.

kefta (moroccan meatballs)

MEATBALLS
600 g (1 lb 5 oz) minced (ground) lamb
1 tablespoon ground ginger
1 tablespoon ground coriander
60 g (2¼ oz/1 cup) breadcrumbs (preferably from day-old bread)
1 tablespoon sea salt

TOMATO SAUCE
2 tablespoons olive oil
1 red onion, thinly sliced
2 garlic cloves, finely chopped
1 tablespoon ras el hanout
125 ml (4 fl oz/½ cup) red wine
400 g (14 oz) tin chopped tomatoes
1 handful coriander (cilantro) leaves and stems, roughly chopped
1 handful flat-leaf (Italian) parsley leaves, roughly chopped

380 g (13½ oz/2 cups) instant couscous
a pinch of salt

Preheat the oven to 180°C (350°F). Line a baking tray with baking paper. To make the meatballs, put all the ingredients in a large bowl. Using your hands, squeeze the mixture between your fingers until everything is well combined. Put some water in a bowl and use wet hands to divide the meat mixture into 16 equal portions. Roll each portion into a small ball and place on the prepared tray. Cook in the oven for 30 minutes, then remove and cover with a clean kitchen cloth.

To make the tomato sauce, heat the oil in a large, deep frying pan over high heat. Add the onion and garlic and stir-fry for 2–3 minutes, until the onion is soft. Add the ras el hanout and cook until fragrant. Add the wine and cook for a minute or so. Stir in the tomatoes and 125 ml (4 fl oz/½ cup) water and bring to the boil for 10 minutes. Stir in the herbs, then add the meatballs and push them into the sauce. Cover and set aside.

Put the couscous and salt in a bowl. Pour 500 ml (17 fl oz/2 cups) warm tap water over the couscous, stir with a fork, then cover and set aside for 10 minutes. Stir again and cover for another 5 minutes. Gently stir the couscous one final time. Put a few heaped spoonfuls of couscous on each plate, then top with the meatballs and sauce.

 If you have any good-quality dried mint, add 2 teaspoons to the meatball mixture. Some pine nuts would be great in this, too.

These stuffed rolls bear a resemblance to beef olives, which are Scottish in origin. This version, *bragioli*, is Maltese but different variations can be found in Italy, too. The rolls are slowly cooked in a rich tomato and red wine sauce, rendering the beef very tender, and then served with crumbled fresh *ġbejniet*, Maltese cheese made from sheep or goat's milk. If you can't find it, use crumbled ricotta instead.

bragioli
(stuffed beef rolls in tomato sauce)

BEEF ROLLS
4 topside steaks, about 200 g (7 oz) each
400 g (14 oz) minced (ground) pork
2 bacon rashers, finely chopped
2 garlic cloves, finely chopped
2 tablespoons chopped rosemary
2 hard-boiled eggs, chopped
1 tablespoon dried oregano, preferably
    Greek oregano (rigani)
1 tablespoon olive oil

SAUCE
2 tablespoons olive oil
1 onion, chopped
2 garlic cloves, chopped
750 ml (26 fl oz/3 cups) tomato passata
    (puréed tomatoes)
1 tablespoon tomato paste (concentrated purée)
250 ml (9 fl oz/1 cup) red wine

100 g (3½ oz) soft Maltese cheese (ġbejniet)
    or fresh ricotta cheese
grilled crusty bread, to serve

To make the beef rolls, lay a piece of plastic food wrap on a chopping board or work surface. Pound the steaks until 5 mm (¼ inch) thick all over, then cut them in half to give eight pieces of meat. Set aside.

Combine the pork, bacon, garlic, rosemary and chopped eggs in a bowl. Season with sea salt and freshly ground black pepper. Using your hands, squeeze the mixture between your fingers for a couple of minutes until everything is well combined.

Using wet hands, form about 60 g (2¼ oz/¼ cup) of the pork mixture into a small sausage and put onto the centre of a piece of beef. Roll the beef into a log to enclose the filling and then secure in place with a toothpick. Repeat with all the beef pieces and pork mixture. Sprinkle the oregano over each beef roll.

Heat the oil in a frying pan over medium heat and cook the beef rolls for 8–10 minutes, turning often until well browned all over. Remove the pan from the heat and set aside.

To make the sauce, heat the oil in a large heavy-based saucepan over high heat. Add the onion and stir-fry for 4–5 minutes, until soft. Add the garlic and cook, stirring, for 1 minute. Add the passata, tomato paste and wine and season with salt and pepper. Bring to the boil, then reduce the heat to a low simmer.

Put the beef rolls in the sauce and pour in any pan juices. Gently move the rolls around in the saucepan so they are covered by the sauce. Cover the pan and cook over low heat for 1 hour, or until the beef is very tender.

Serve the beef rolls with the Maltese cheese crumbled over the top of each roll, with crusty bread to mop up the sauce and with your favourite green salad.

NEXT TIME *Replace the bacon with 100 g (3½ oz) chopped pancetta. The pancetta will add extra spice as it is traditionally made with lots of freshly ground black pepper.*

bragioli (stuffed beef rolls in tomato sauce) *page 134*

Numerous versions of stir-fried minced (ground) meat can be found all over Southeast Asia—Thai and Laotian *larb* springs to mind. This may be a less well known, Indian version. That said, *keema* is also popular in Pakistan, Bangladesh, Afghanistan and Nepal. While rice may be the obvious choice as a side, this spiced beef is delicious wrapped in soft flatbread.

beef keema
(indian beef mince curry)

500 g (1 lb 2 oz) minced (ground) beef

260 g (9¼ oz/1 cup) plain yoghurt

1 teaspoon salt

2 tablespoons vegetable oil

2 onions, finely chopped

1 tablespoon finely chopped garlic

1 tablespoon finely grated fresh ginger

2 green cardamom pods

2 large green chillies, finely chopped

1 tablespoon ground cumin

1 tablespoon ground coriander

1 tablespoon fennel seeds

1 teaspoon ground turmeric

1 teaspoon chilli powder

140 g (5 oz/1 cup) frozen peas

25 g (1 oz/½ cup) roughly chopped coriander (cilantro) leaves

Put the beef, yoghurt and salt in a bowl and stir to combine well. Set aside for 1 hour.

Heat the oil in a large frying pan over high heat. Add the onions and stir-fry for 8–10 minutes, until the onions are really soft and aromatic.

Stir in the garlic, ginger, cardamom and chillies and cook for 2–3 minutes, until aromatic. Stir in the cumin, coriander, fennel, turmeric and chilli powder and cook for 2–3 minutes, until the mixture is dark and fragrant.

Add the beef mixture, stirring with a wooden spoon to break up any large pieces of meat. Add the peas and cook for 15 minutes, stirring often, until the beef is brown and any liquid in the pan has evaporated. Stir in the coriander. Serve with basmati rice or warm Indian flatbread.

NEXT TIME *Using minced (ground) beef for this recipe keeps the costs down, but if you cook this and find you really like it and want to explore other options, try it with minced (ground) lamb.*

This might sound odd, but I really like either the beef or lamb version of this with a fried egg on top for brunch.

One look at a Thai curry recipe may have you running the other way. The list of ingredients is often quite long and the last thing you want is to put so much time and effort into making something you aren't happy with. That won't happen here.

gaeng kiew wan moo
(thai green curry of pork)

400 ml (14 fl oz) tin coconut cream
500 g (1 lb 2 oz) pork scotch neck, cut into 2–3 cm (3/4–11/4 inch) cubes
2 teaspoons sugar
2 teaspoons fish sauce
400 ml (14 fl oz) tin coconut milk
6 kaffir lime leaves
1 handful Thai basil leaves
100 g (31/2 oz/2/3 cup) tinned sliced bamboo shoots

GREEN CURRY PASTE
1 tablespoon Thai shrimp paste with soy bean oil
6 large green chillies, chopped
4 green bird's eye chillies, chopped
1 red onion, chopped
4 garlic cloves, chopped
1 lemongrass stem, pale part only, chopped
1 large handful coriander (cilantro) leaves, chopped
1 teaspoon ground coriander
1 teaspoon ground cumin
1/2 teaspoon ground white pepper
60 ml (2 fl oz/1/4 cup) boiling water

To make the green curry paste, put all the paste ingredients in a food processor and process until smooth and pale green. Set aside.

Put 250 ml (9 fl oz/1 cup) of the coconut cream in a heavy-based saucepan and bring to the boil. Cook until the coconut cream is rapidly boiling and the surface is pooled with bubbles. Stir the curry paste into the coconut cream and cook for 10 minutes over medium heat, stirring often, until olive green in colour.

Add the pork and cook for 8–10 minutes, until the pork is no longer pink. Stir in the sugar and fish sauce and cook for 2–3 minutes, until aromatic and dark. Stir in the coconut milk and remaining coconut cream. Cover and cook over low heat for 1 hour, or until the pork is tender. Stir in the lime leaves, basil and bamboo shoots. Serve with steamed jasmine rice.

NEXT TIME *You could use chicken here instead of the pork (keep in mind that chicken will cook quicker than pork) and beef chuck would work well too–the cooking time for beef is about the same as the pork.*

shindig

When we have to cook for others, we want food that's easy to prepare without compromising on flavour—effortless food that will still impress. After all, entertaining is also about spending time with your guests, not endless hours chained to the stove.

Recipes for tray-baked pizza, Spanish-inspired mackerel and an Armenian cheesy lasagne will guarantee flavour in every mouthful. Served with a crisp green salad, these recipes are great for summer entertaining. Or if it's winter meals you're after, try dishes such as the vegetable korma curry or beef cheek stew topped with crispy French fries.

And then there are times when you're asked to 'bring a plate'. The eggplant parmigiana and roast beef salad can be cooked beforehand, wrapped in foil and taken with you—perfect for picnics, too.

Any type of shindig. This chapter has you covered.

Tequila really imparts the most amazing flavour when cooked. We often cook with wine and beer, and I've seen vodka used in a pasta sauce, so using tequila isn't that strange when you think about it. The tequila cooks down to a deeply sweet flavour and the inclusion of parmesan adds to the whole umami (savoury flavour) experience. And the lime? Well, it just brings the whole thing together.

parmesan, tequila and lime pork

1 tablespoon olive oil
1 large brown onion, sliced into thin wedges
3 garlic cloves, chopped
1 teaspoon dried oregano
1 kg (2 lb 4 oz) pork neck, cut into 4-5 pieces
250 ml (9 fl oz/1 cup) tequila
125 ml (4 fl oz/½ cup) lime juice

60 ml (2 fl oz/¼ cup) sriracha sauce
45 g (1½ oz/¼ cup, lightly packed) light brown sugar
25 g (1 oz/¼ cup) grated parmesan cheese
12 soft wheat tortillas, warmed
1 Lebanese (short) cucumber, sliced with a peeler into thin ribbons

Preheat the oven to 180°C (350°F). Heat the oil in a flameproof casserole dish over high heat. Add the onion, season well with sea salt and freshly ground black pepper, and stir-fry for 8–10 minutes. You want the onions to be really golden and starting to char around the edges. Add the garlic and oregano and cook for 1 minute.

Add the pork pieces to the dish and cook for about 10 minutes, turning the pork over every couple of minutes, until well browned. Stir in the tequila, lime juice, sriracha and brown sugar, turning the pork pieces around in the dish to coat in the sauce.

Sprinkle the parmesan over the pork, then cover with a tight-fitting lid or foil. Transfer the dish to the oven and cook for 1 hour. Then turn the pork over, cover again and cook for a further 1 hour. Remove from the oven and set aside, still covered, for 15–20 minutes. This will allow the flavours to really develop and the pork to tenderise. Use kitchen tongs to shred the pork; it should fall apart easily. Serve the shredded pork wrapped in the warm tortillas and topped with the cucumber ribbons.

NEXT TIME *Replace the pork with 1 kg (2 lb 4 oz) chuck steak, cut into large chunks. For an extra smoky flavour, replace the sriracha sauce with puréed chipotle or 1 tablespoon smoked Spanish paprika.*

SHINDIG

A spiedie is an abbreviation of the Italian *spiedini*—cubes of marinated meat that are skewered and then grilled. The skewers are laid on an open roll, the roll is then closed and helps to secure the pieces of meat while the skewer is removed. Sounds good? Let's get cracking!

spiedies with roast garlic mayo

2 kg (4 lb 8 oz) lamb leg meat, fat trimmed
2 tablespoons olive oil
60 ml (2 fl oz/¼ cup) white wine vinegar
4 garlic cloves, roughly chopped
2 teaspoons dried oregano
7 g (¼ oz/¼ cup) chopped flat-leaf (Italian)
    parsley
1 teaspoon chilli flakes
1 teaspoon sea salt
12 bread rolls, halved

ROAST GARLIC MAYONNAISE
1 large garlic bulb
2 teaspoons olive oil
350 g (12 oz/1½ cups) good-quality mayonnaise
1 tablespoon dijon mustard

Cut the lamb into smallish cubes, no bigger than 3 cm (1¼ inches), and put into a ceramic or glass bowl. Add the oil, vinegar, garlic, oregano, parsley, chilli, salt and a generous grinding of black pepper. Using your hands, toss the lamb in the marinade to coat well. Cover and refrigerate for 3–6 hours or preferably overnight (remove the lamb from the fridge 30 minutes before cooking).

To make the roast garlic mayonnaise, preheat the oven to 200°C (400°F). Put the garlic bulb on a piece of foil and drizzle over the oil. Loosely wrap the garlic in the foil and sit on the centre shelf of the oven. Roast for 25–30 minutes, until the garlic is soft. When the garlic is cool enough to handle, cut in half crossways. Squeeze the softened cloves into the bowl of a food processor. Add the mayonnaise and mustard and process until smooth. Transfer the garlic mayonnaise to a container and refrigerate.

Soak 12 bamboo skewers in cold water for 30 minutes before using. Thread pieces of lamb onto each skewer—each skewer should fit around five to seven pieces of lamb.

Preheat the barbecue grill or hotplate to high. Alternatively, cook this inside using a large frying pan over high heat. Cook the lamb skewers for 6 minutes, then turn them over and cook for a further 4–5 minutes, until the lamb is golden all over but still slightly pink in the centre. Cook longer if you prefer well-done lamb. Transfer to a plate, cover with foil and rest for 5–10 minutes.

Place the bread rolls on the barbecue hotplate or under a hot grill (broiler) and toast until golden. Spread the rolls with a generous amount of garlic mayo. Lay a skewer on each roll, close the roll and hold it while you pull the skewer out.

NEXT TIME *Use fish here instead of the lamb, but choose the fish wisely. Fish that has been frozen may stick to the cooking surface and delicate fish will fall apart too much when cooked. Fresh, firm or oily fish fillets, such as mackerel, tuna or kingfish, are the best options.*

chicken shawarma with **home-made flatbreads** *page 150*

This recipe uses the flavour of authentic shawarma, but without the traditional cooking technique of shaving meat slices from a vertical spit—not the most user-friendly technique in the average home. The chicken here is marinated in an aromatic concoction of spices, then simply cooked off in the oven.

I've also included a recipe for flatbreads. You could run out and buy some ready-made flatbreads if you prefer, but there really is nothing like bread when it is home-made. The breads can be made in advance—to reheat them, wrap in foil and place in a low oven until warmed through.

chicken shawarma with home-made flatbreads

8 boneless, skinless chicken thigh fillets
2 red onions, thinly sliced
1 tablespoon light olive oil
400 g (14 oz/1½ cups) plain yoghurt
1 handful mint leaves, finely chopped
pickled turnips (preferably Lebanese), to serve

MARINADE
80 ml (2½ fl oz/⅓ cup) light olive oil
80 ml (2½ fl oz/⅓ cup) lemon juice
6 garlic cloves, chopped
1 teaspoon ground turmeric
1 teaspoon ground ginger
1 teaspoon chilli powder
1 tablespoon sweet paprika
1 tablespoon ground cumin
1 large handful flat-leaf (Italian) parsley leaves,
    chopped

FLATBREADS
½ teaspoon bicarbonate of soda (baking soda)
260 g (9¼ oz/1 cup) plain yoghurt
300 g (10½ oz/2 cups) self-raising flour,
    plus extra for dusting
½ teaspoon sea salt
1 teaspoon sugar

To make the marinade, combine all the ingredients in a large bowl. Put the chicken in the bowl and use your hands to rub the marinade all over the chicken. Cover and refrigerate for 6 hours or overnight (remove the chicken from the fridge 30 minutes before cooking).

To make the flatbreads, combine the bicarbonate of soda and yoghurt in a bowl and set aside for 5–10 minutes, or until the yoghurt looks frothy.

Combine the flour, salt and sugar in a bowl and make a well in the centre. Add the yoghurt to the well and use your hands to combine—the dough will be sticky and wet. Work the dough until smooth and shiny. Cover with plastic wrap and set aside for 30 minutes, or until the dough has almost doubled in size.

Divide the dough into eight portions, then form each portion into a ball. On a lightly floured surface, roll each ball into a flat circle, about 20 cm (8 inches) in diameter. Place the dough rounds on a lightly greased piece of baking paper, then cover with a cloth or plastic wrap. Set aside for about 30 minutes, or until slightly risen.

To cook the flatbreads, heat a large non-stick frying pan or a barbecue hotplate over high heat. Cook the breads for a couple of minutes each side, until golden. Transfer to a plate and cover with foil to keep warm.

To cook the chicken, preheat the oven to 220°C (425°F). Spread the onions over the base of a baking dish and drizzle over the oil. Put the chicken and marinade on top of the onions, spreading the chicken out to avoid overlapping. Cook in the oven for 20 minutes, then turn the chicken over and cook for a further 20 minutes, or until the chicken is golden and aromatic and the onions are tender.

Transfer the chicken to a chopping board and put the onions in a bowl. Thinly slice the chicken and place in a serving bowl along with any cooking juices. Combine the yoghurt and mint in a separate bowl. Serve the chicken in the flatbreads with the onions, pickles and minted yoghurt.

NEXT TIME *Any left-over chicken can be used to make a quick and easy bastilla (Moroccan chicken pie). Shred the chicken and put it in a ceramic pie dish. Cover with several layers of filo pastry, which have been brushed with melted butter. Bake in a 180°C (350°F) oven until golden. Combine 2 teaspoons icing (confectioners') sugar and ½ teaspoon ground cinnamon and finely sift over the filo.*

The *banh mi* war wages in my home town of Sydney. It seems as though every suburb has at least one Vietnamese bakery whipping up their version of traditional French pastries, as well as small baguette-type rolls, *banh mi*, filled with all sorts of pork products, chicken, salads, herbs and pickled carrots. As I stood in line one weekend, waiting my turn to order, I realised this wasn't the type of food you make for one or two. This is a very clever and tasty way to feed lots of people.

banh mi banquet

PICKLED CARROTS
2 carrots
1 teaspoon salt
1 teaspoon sugar
60 ml (2 fl oz/¼ cup) rice vinegar

2 large handfuls coriander (cilantro) leaves
   and stems
6 spring onions (scallions), roughly chopped
5 cm (2 inch) piece fresh ginger, thinly sliced
1 tablespoon salt
2 boneless, skinless chicken breast fillets
3 garlic cloves, chopped
2 lemongrass stems, pale parts only, chopped
2 tablespoons oyster sauce
½ teaspoon ground white pepper
500 g (1 lb 2 oz) pork neck, sliced into 1 cm
   (½ inch) thick steaks
1 tablespoon vegetable oil
2 tomatoes, sliced
2 Lebanese (short) cucumbers, thinly sliced
   lengthways into ribbons
2 large red chillies, thinly sliced
1 butter lettuce, leaves separated
235 g (8½ oz/1 cup) whole egg mayonnaise
8 bread rolls, preferably Vietnamese banh mi
butter, to serve

To make the pickled carrots, use a box grater to thickly grate the carrots into a bowl. Add the salt and stir the carrots around to coat in the salt. Leave for 10 minutes. Squeeze out as much of the salty liquid as possible, then transfer the carrot to a bowl. Stir in the sugar and vinegar, then cover and refrigerate.

Put half the coriander and half the spring onions in a large saucepan. Add the ginger, salt and 2 litres (70 fl oz/8 cups) cold water. Bring to the boil and then continue to boil for 5 minutes, to allow the flavours to develop. Add the chicken breasts, then remove the pan from the heat. Cover the pan and refrigerate until cool. Remove the chicken from the poaching liquid, discarding the liquid. Use your fingers to shred the chicken meat into a bowl and refrigerate.

Put the remaining coriander, remaining spring onions, garlic, lemongrass, oyster sauce and white pepper in a food processor and process to form a thick paste. Scrape the paste into a large bowl. Add the pork and toss to coat in the paste. Set aside for 30 minutes.

To cook the pork, heat the oil in a frying pan or barbecue hotplate over high heat. Cook the pork for 3 minutes on each side, or until dark golden. Remove and allow to rest for 10 minutes. Slice the pork across the grain into thin strips and transfer to a plate.

To serve, place all the remaining filling ingredients in bowls or on platters and arrange on a table with the bread rolls and butter on the side. Each person can assemble their own roll, using whatever ingredients they like.

NEXT TIME *I am a big fan of prawn (shrimp) sandwiches. Put 24 large peeled and deveined prawns in a bowl with 1 tablespoon vegetable oil, 2 tablespoons fish sauce, 2 finely chopped lemongrass stems (pale parts only), 1 teaspoon finely chopped chilli and 2 finely chopped garlic cloves. Toss to coat in the marinade, then cook the prawns in a chargrill pan or on the barbecue hotplate until pink and curled up. Sprinkle with some ground white pepper. Serve the prawns in a bowl and add to the bread rolls as an addition or alternative to the chicken and pork.*

banh mi banquet *page 152*

tray pizza with ale dough   page 156

The tricky thing about making any pizza is the dough—the toppings are really just personal add-ons. It's a bit like telling someone how much butter to put on their toast. The topping ingredients given here are just a suggestion, albeit a very tasty one. The dough is where the real money is. Using beer greatly adds to the flavour and texture of the dough. You can roll the dough into conventional rounds, but I like to stretch and roll the dough on a large baking tray—easier for when feeding a crowd.

tray pizza with ale dough

ALE DOUGH
300 g (10½ oz/2 cups) self-raising flour
¼ teaspoon bicarbonate of soda (baking soda)
½ teaspoon salt
½ teaspoon sugar
250 ml (9 fl oz/1 cup) India pale ale, at room
    temperature
1 tablespoon olive oil

500 g (1 lb 2 oz) jar tomato Napolitana pasta
    sauce
2 teaspoons chilli flakes
240 g (8½ oz/4 cups) thinly sliced Swiss brown
    mushrooms
2 red onions, thinly sliced
460 g (1 lb/2 cups) fresh ricotta cheese
500 g (1 lb 2 oz/4 cups) grated mozzarella
    cheese
12 slices jamón or prosciutto, roughly torn
60 g (2¼ oz/2 cups, lightly packed) basil leaves

To make the ale dough, combine the flour, bicarbonate of soda, salt and sugar in a bowl. Add the beer and oil and mix with a large spoon to make a soft and sticky batter. Use floured hands to form the dough into a ball. Transfer to a well-floured surface and knead for 4–5 minutes, until smooth. Form the dough into a ball and put into a clean bowl. Cover with a clean kitchen cloth and leave in a warm spot for 30 minutes, or until slightly puffed.

Preheat the oven to 220°C (425°F). Lightly grease a baking tray with olive oil. If you have two trays, make the second pizza at the same time; otherwise, make and cook them one at a time.

Divide the dough in half and put one half back in the bowl. On a well-floured surface, roll the dough ball into a rectangle shape, roughly the size of the baking tray. Transfer the dough to the tray and use your fingers to stretch and press the dough up the sides of the tray a little, to form a raised edge.

Spread half the pasta sauce over the dough, then sprinkle over half the chilli flakes and top with half the mushrooms and onion. Dollop half of the ricotta over the top and then scatter over half of the mozzarella.

Bake in the oven for 20–25 minutes, until the dough is risen and golden and the cheese is bubbling hot.

Use a pair of kitchen tongs to grab one end of the pizza and slide it onto a chopping board. Scatter the jamón and basil over the top. Cut into small pieces and serve.

NEXT TIME *Make a meat-lover's version. Stir 60 ml (2 fl oz/¼ cup) barbecue sauce into the pasta sauce. Use chopped barbecued (rotisserie) chicken, chopped bacon and sliced pepperoni to replace the jamón, and replace the ricotta cheese with more mozzarella.*

Gado gado is an Indonesian dish of blanched or steamed vegetables, tofu and boiled eggs topped with a delicious peanut sauce. I stumbled upon the idea of using roasted vegetables instead of blanched ones when I had some cooked vegetables left over from a roast chicken dinner. Traditionally the blanched vegetables are refreshed in cold water and serve chilled, but I prefer the veggies to be cooked and served warm. The really great thing about this dish is that it's transportable. Cook the veggies beforehand, and keep the peanut sauce in a separate container, then plate everything up when you get there. Typically the peanut sauce is served on top of the vegetables—not always the most appetising of presentations. I've done the reverse here, with the peanut sauce served underneath the delicious vegetables.

roasted vegetable gado gado

PEANUT SAUCE
1 tablespoon vegetable oil
1 red onion, chopped
4 garlic cloves, finely chopped
2 large red chillies, roughly chopped
1 teaspoon shrimp paste
4 kaffir lime leaves, roughly chopped
260 g (9¼ oz/1 cup) crunchy peanut butter
1 tablespoon light brown sugar
400 ml (14 fl oz) tin coconut cream
1 tablespoon kecap manis

2 tablespoons olive oil
400 g (14 oz) orange sweet potato, cut into
    3–4 cm (1¼–1½ inch) cubes
8 kipfler (fingerling) potatoes, washed and
    halved lengthways
200 g (7 oz) green beans, trimmed
½ head cauliflower, broken into small florets
½ Chinese cabbage (wong bok), chopped into
    2 cm (¾ inch) thick slices
100 g (3½ oz/¾ cup) bean sprouts
200 g (7 oz) ready-made fried tofu, sliced
    (see Next Time)
6 hard-boiled eggs, peeled and halved

To make the peanut sauce, heat the vegetable oil in a frying pan over medium heat. Add the onion and stir-fry for 2–3 minutes, until softened. Add the garlic and chillies and cook for 1 minute. Stir in the shrimp paste, lime leaves, peanut butter, brown sugar, coconut cream, kecap manis and 1 tablespoon water. Cook for 5 minutes, or until the sauce has thickened and is caramel coloured. Remove from the heat and set aside to cool for 10 minutes.

Transfer the mixture to a food processor and process to make a smooth paste. Refrigerate until needed.

Preheat the oven to 180°C (350°F). Put the olive oil in a large bowl and season with sea salt and freshly ground black pepper. Put the sweet potatoes, potatoes, beans, cauliflower and cabbage in the bowl. Toss the vegetables around to coat in the oil. Tumble onto two baking trays and roast in the oven for 40 minutes, or until all the vegetables are tender.

Add the bean sprouts and tofu to the vegetables and roast for a further 5 minutes, or until warmed through.

To serve, spread the peanut sauce over the base of a large platter or divide it among individual plates. Pile the vegetable mixture and boiled eggs on top. Serve warm or at room temperature.

NEXT TIME *This recipe uses fried tofu, which can be bought ready-to-go from Asian food stores. However, I also really like chargrilled or barbecued tofu in this. Cut a 300 g (10½ oz) block of firm tofu into 1 cm (½ inch) thick slices. If you have the time, marinate the tofu in some light soy sauce and grated fresh ginger. Cook on a lightly greased chargrill pan or barbecue hotplate until golden, and serve with the gado gado.*

roasted vegetable gado gado *page 158*

We might not think of curries as party or entertaining food, but they are a great way to feed a gang. And it's an ideal way to use up those rather sad-looking veggies in the crisper drawer of your fridge: the less-than-fresh potato, the limpish beans or the cauli that's about to lose its vigour. Combine these vegetables with a few pantry basics and you'll have the dreamiest of korma curries. Put the curry and a bowl of steamed rice on the table and let everyone help themselves.

crisper vegetable korma

2 potatoes, quartered
250 g (9 oz/2 cups) trimmed
    and quartered green beans
1/2 head cauliflower, broken into
    small florets
50 g (1³⁄₄ oz) butter
500 ml (17 fl oz/2 cups) thickened
    (whipping) cream
40 g (1¹⁄₂ oz/¹⁄₄ cup) roasted, salted
    cashews
1 small handful coriander
    (cilantro) sprigs

KORMA PASTE
1 brown onion, roughly chopped
1 tablespoon grated fresh ginger
4 garlic cloves, finely chopped
150 g (5¹⁄₂ oz/1 cup) roasted,
    salted cashews
1 teaspoon cumin seeds
1 teaspoon ground coriander
1/2 teaspoon chilli powder
1/2 teaspoon ground turmeric
1 tablespoon tomato paste
    (concentrated purée)

Bring a large saucepan of salted water to the boil. Add the potatoes, beans and cauliflower, then cover with a lid and remove from the heat. Set aside, covered, for 15 minutes, or until the vegetables are just tender. Drain and set aside.

Meanwhile, to make the korma paste, put all the paste ingredients in a food processor and process until smooth. Set aside.

Heat the butter in a large saucepan over medium heat. When the butter starts to sizzle, add the korma paste and stir-fry for 4–5 minutes, until the paste is darker in colour and aromatic. Stir in the cream and gently simmer for 5 minutes. Add all the vegetables and stir to combine, then reduce the heat to low and simmer gently for 10 minutes, to combine all the flavours in a thick, creamy sauce. Scatter the cashews and coriander over the top and serve with steamed rice.

NEXT TIME *Why not add some prawns (shrimp)? After you have simmered the vegetables in the sauce, stir in 16 large, peeled and deveined raw prawns. Cook gently for just a few minutes, until the prawns are pink, curled up and cooked through.*

An Italian classic, eggplant parmigiana is pure comfort food. And there is no meat in sight, which means it can be ready to eat with very little cooking time. Its simplicity is reminiscent of a good pizza: only a few ingredients are needed but these need to be top quality. Look for firm, shiny eggplants (aubergines) and only use the best quality cheese. It is said this classic dish comes from Campania, the southwest region of Italy, which has Naples, the home of pizza, as its capital.

eggplant parmigiana

500 ml (17 fl oz/2 cups) light olive oil
4 garlic cloves, thinly sliced
1 teaspoon chilli flakes
1 litre (35 fl oz/4 cups) tomato passata
    (puréed tomatoes)
1 teaspoon dried oregano, preferably
    Greek oregano (rigani)
3 large eggplants (aubergines)
4 eggs
50 g (1¾ oz/½ cup) finely grated pecorino
    cheese
50 g (1¾ oz/½ cup) finely grated parmesan
    cheese
grilled Italian ciabatta, to serve

Heat 60 ml (2 fl oz/¼ cup) of the oil in a saucepan over medium heat. Add the garlic and chilli flakes and cook for 1–2 minutes, until the garlic is fragrant and softened but not brown. Add the passata and oregano, season with sea salt and freshly ground black pepper and cook for a further 10 minutes. Remove the pan from the heat and set aside.

Preheat the oven to 180°C (350°F). Trim the ends off the eggplants and discard. Cut about 5 mm (¼ inch) off each side of the eggplants and discard. Now slice the eggplants lengthways into 5 mm (¼ inch) thick slices. Set aside.

Lightly beat the eggs in a wide bowl with 2 tablespoons of pecorino and 2 tablespoons of parmesan. Combine the remaining cheeses in one bowl.

Heat a little of the remaining oil in a large frying pan over medium–high heat. Working in batches and adding more oil as needed, dip the eggplant slices into the egg mixture and fry for 2–3 minutes, until golden.

Pour about 125 ml (4 fl oz/½ cup) of the tomato sauce into a 20 x 30 cm (8 x 12 inch) baking dish. Spread the sauce evenly over the base of the dish. Arrange a layer of eggplant over the tomato sauce and sprinkle one-third of the combined cheeses over the top. Repeat with a layer of sauce, the remaining eggplant and one-third of cheese. Finish with a final layer of sauce and cheese.

Cook in the oven for 40 minutes, or until golden and bubbling hot. Allow to cool slightly before cutting. Serve a square of the eggplant parmigiana between two slices of ciabatta.

NEXT TIME *Rather than using cheese, add some fresh basil leaves between the layers of eggplant (aubergine). And make a topping by combining 230 g (8 oz/1 cup) fresh ricotta cheese, 50 g (1¾ oz/½ cup) finely grated parmesan cheese and ½ teaspoon ground cinnamon in a bowl. Season well and spoon this mixture over the top of the eggplant before baking.*

eggplant parmigiana *page 164*

I love Asian-style beef salads, but lately they seem to be everywhere. I wanted this recipe to take us back to the basics, to the old-school beef salads from days gone by. It's also perfect food to take on a picnic. The steak can be cooked at home, wrapped in foil and sliced just before serving.

roast beef salad

750 g (1 lb 10 oz) sirloin steak
1 tablespoon Worcestershire sauce
1 teaspoon sea salt
1 teaspoon freshly ground black pepper
125 ml (4 fl oz/½ cup) olive oil
300 g (10½ oz) kipfler (fingerling) potatoes,
    or any waxy potatoes, cleaned
6 roma (plum) tomatoes, halved
3 small red onions, peeled and sliced

SALSA VERDE (GREEN SAUCE)
2 handfuls basil leaves
2 handfuls mint leaves
2 handfuls flat-leaf (Italian) parsley leaves
2 spring onions (scallions), chopped
2 garlic cloves, chopped
2 large dill pickles, chopped
185 ml (6 fl oz/¾ cup) light olive oil

Put the steak on a plate, drizzle over the Worcestershire sauce, then season both sides of the meat with the salt and pepper. Set aside for about 1 hour at room temperature. If you are super organised, this can be done a day in advance; just keep the steak in the fridge, uncovered, and remove 30 minutes before cooking.

Heat 2 tablespoons of the oil in a heavy-based frying pan over high heat. When the oil is smoking hot, carefully put the steak in the pan and cook for 3 minutes on each side. Reduce the heat to medium and cook for a further 3 minutes on each side. Place the steak on a plate and leave to cool to room temperature. Again, this can be done a day in advance; just keep the steak refrigerated, if so.

Preheat the oven to 180°C (350°F). Put the potatoes, tomatoes and onions in a small baking dish. You want the vegetables to fit snugly. Pour the remaining oil over the vegetables and season well. Cook in the oven for 1 hour, or until the vegetables are very tender. Remove from the oven and allow to cool in the dish.

To make the salsa verde, put all the herbs, spring onions, garlic and pickles in a food processor and process for just a few seconds. Add the oil and process to make a smooth, vibrant green sauce.

Tumble all the vegetables onto a large serving platter. Thinly slice the beef and lay the strips over the vegetables. Serve with the salsa verde.

 Instead of using sirloin steak, use the same weight in boneless lamb leg steaks, lamb backstraps or loin fillets.

This is a gooey and tasty take on the traditional meat lasagne. Although this cheesy version is very traditional in its own right—it's an Armenian cheese lasagne, or *sou boreg*—what I really wanted here was to create the lasagne version of four-cheese pizza or pasta. I've used blue cheese and ricotta, but you could replace either one with cottage cheese.

And best not to serve this piping hot because it is too sloppy. This could sit for 30–45 minutes after it is taken out of the oven, which makes this an even better dish to make for a crowd or to take to a mate's place.

four-cheese lasagne

400 g (14 oz) fresh lasagne sheets
100 g (3½ oz) butter
35 g (1¼ oz/¼ cup) plain (all-purpose) flour
750 ml (26 fl oz/3 cups) milk
60 g (2¼ oz/½ cup) crumbled blue cheese
400 g (14 oz/1⅔ cups) fresh ricotta cheese
100 g (3½ oz/1 cup) finely grated parmesan
    cheese
1 egg
¼ teaspoon freshly grated nutmeg
125 g (4½ oz/1 cup) grated firm mozzarella
    cheese
½ teaspoon sweet paprika

Bring a large saucepan of cold water to the boil and add a generous pinch of salt. When the water returns to the boil, add the lasagne sheets and, working in batches of three or four at a time, cook for 2–3 minutes, until slippery and just *al dente* (the pasta will have more time to cook in the oven). Rinse under cold water and drain well.

Put the butter in a saucepan over medium heat. When the butter has melted and starts to sizzle, add the flour and stir to make a smooth, thick paste. Cook for 2–3 minutes, until the paste is pale golden. Slowly add the milk, stirring constantly, and cook for 4–5 minutes to make a smooth, thick white sauce. Set aside.

Preheat the oven to 180°C (350°F). Lightly grease a 20 x 30 cm (8 x 12 inch) baking dish. Spoon 60 ml (2 fl oz/¼ cup) of the white sauce into the dish and spread it out to cover the base. This will prevent the pasta from sticking. Top with a single layer of pasta. It's fine if they overlap slightly, but trim them if necessary—you don't want double layers of pasta.

Scatter the blue cheese evenly over the pasta, then dollop with another 60 ml (2 fl oz/¼ cup) of the sauce. Arrange another layer of pasta over the top. Combine the ricotta, half the parmesan, the egg and nutmeg in a bowl. Spoon the ricotta mixture over the pasta. Top with another layer of pasta.

Add the remaining parmesan and all the mozzarella to the white sauce in the saucepan. Stir to combine, then spread the cheesy sauce over the final layer of pasta. Sprinkle the paprika evenly over the top. Sit the baking dish on a large tray in case the sauce bubbles over, then transfer to the oven and bake for 45 minutes, or until the top is golden and the lasagne is bubbling hot.

Leave the lasagne to cool a little, then cut into squares and serve with a green salad. This is also delicious served cold, cut into smaller squares as a snack.

 Add 2–3 tablespoons sun-dried tomato pesto to the white sauce, or stir some fresh basil and baby spinach leaves through the sauce.

four-cheese lasagne *page 170*

This is one of those dishes that works year round. It's light and fresh for summer when it can be cooked in advance and served at room temperature, and the warm spices and sweet dried fruit make it perfect for serving on colder days too. This is easy to transport as well—great for when you've been asked to 'bring a plate'. Just wrap the whole pot in cooking foil to keep the heat in.

fragrant chicken and almond pilaf

1 barbecued (rotisserie) chicken
2 tablespoons olive oil
1 red onion, sliced
2 garlic cloves, chopped
100 g (3½ oz/¾ cup) slivered almonds
300 g (10½ oz/1½ cups) long-grain rice
1 teaspoon ground ginger
1 teaspoon ground cinnamon
2 teaspoons ground cumin
120 g (4¼ oz/⅔ cup) raisins
120 g (4¼ oz/⅔ cup) dried apricots, sliced
750 ml (26 fl oz/3 cups) chicken stock
1 large handful coriander (cilantro) leaves and
    stems, roughly chopped

Start by using your hands to pull off large pieces of skin and meat from the chicken. I usually snack on the wings while I'm doing this. Thinly slice the skin and pull the chicken into thin strips and put in a bowl.

Heat the oil in a large heavy-based saucepan over high heat. Add the onion and stir-fry for 4–5 minutes, until softened. Stir in the garlic and cook for 1 minute, or until aromatic, then stir in the almonds and cook for 1 minute, or until the nuts have a hint of colour.

Add the rice and stir for a couple of minutes, until each grain is glossy and the rice has a nutty aroma. Now add the ginger, cinnamon, cumin, raisins and apricots. Cook for a minute or so, just until the spices are fragrant. Add all the chicken to the pan and stir well to combine with the rice.

Add the stock, taking care as it will sizzle when it hits the hot pan. Stir quickly a few times to remove any bits stuck to the bottom of the pan, then reduce the heat to low and cover the pan with a tight-fitting lid. Cook for 25 minutes, leaving the lid on; this will keep the heat in and steam the rice.

Remove the pan from the heat and leave for 15 minutes, again without removing the lid. Before serving, stir the coriander through the rice.

NEXT TIME *A vegetarian version of this pilaf requires very little effort. Replace the chicken with a combination of vegetables such as eggplant (aubergine), zucchini (courgette) and sweet potato. Cut the vegetables into large bite-sized pieces and toss them in a little olive oil, sea salt and chilli flakes. Tumble onto a baking tray and roast in a 180°C (350°F) oven until golden and tender. Cook the rice as per the recipe and stir the roasted vegetables through the cooked rice.*

I'm not entirely sure what a buffalo wing is or why a chicken wing has anything to do with a buffalo. I have had many a discussion with beer aficionados on the subject—beer drinkers seem to be particularly partial to the buffalo. And, after much research, I've concluded that the buffalo wing can be many things to many people. The common thread, however, is that there must always be heat (in the form of chilli) and tang (in the form of vinegar). Chicken wings are certainly one of Mother Nature's more clever contributions to the world of finger food.

sriracha buffalo wings with blue cheese slaw

BLUE CHEESE SLAW
125 g (4¹/₂ oz/1 cup) crumbled blue cheese
2 tablespoons fresh lemon juice
85 g (3 oz/¹/₃ cup) good-quality mayonnaise
¹/₂ teaspoon freshly ground black pepper
1 celery stalk, finely chopped
2 carrots, coarsely grated
3 spring onions (scallions), thinly sliced
    diagonally
300 g (10¹/₂ oz/4 cups) finely chopped savoy
    cabbage

24 chicken wings, tips removed then halved
300 g (10¹/₂ oz/2 cups) plain (all-purpose) flour
2 teaspoons sea salt
1 teaspoon ground white pepper
1 teaspoon ground cinnamon
60 ml (2 fl oz/¹/₄ cup) sriracha sauce
100 g (3¹/₂ oz) butter
60 ml (2 fl oz/¹/₄ cup) white wine vinegar

To make the blue cheese slaw, combine all the slaw ingredients in a bowl. Cover and refrigerate until needed. This can be done up to a few hours in advance, but no more than that as the slaw will lose its freshness.

Preheat the oven to 220°C (425°F). Put the chicken wings in a large bowl and add the flour, salt, white pepper and cinnamon. Toss the chicken around in the bowl, to coat all over in the flour.

Put the chicken wings on a large baking tray, spreading them out so they don't overlap. Transfer the tray to the oven and cook for 30–35 minutes, until golden and cooked through.

Put the hot chicken wings in a bowl with the sriracha, butter and vinegar. Toss the chicken around to melt the butter and coat the chicken in the buttery sauce. Serve the chicken wings with chilled blue cheese slaw.

NEXT TIME *For a pescetarian version, substitute the chicken with fish. Salmon would be ideal. Cut 4 salmon fillets (about 200 g/7 oz each) into large bite-sized pieces, about 3–4 cm (1¼–1½ inches). Proceed with the recipe as you would with the chicken, but reduce the cooking time to 10–12 minutes.*

sriracha buffalo wings with **blue cheese slaw** *page 176*

baked spanish mackerel   *page 180*

This is just as good for catering for a small group as it is for an intimate dinner. Most domestic ovens should fit three, maybe four, trays, so you could easily make this for sixteen. The important ingredient here is the chorizo. I prefer to use a fairly spicy fresh chorizo. Good-quality chorizo will be embedded with garlic, chilli and smoked paprika, which ensures this dish will be packed with those lovely, warming Spanish flavours. Not-so-good chorizo will be little more than glorified cabanossi.

baked spanish mackerel

60 ml (2 fl oz/¼ cup) olive oil
4 waxy potatoes, chopped
4 mackerel cutlets, about 250 g (9 oz) each
1 large fresh chorizo, about 200 g (7 oz), roughly
    chopped
1 large red onion, thinly sliced
45 g (1½ oz/¼ cup) kalamata olives
1 tablespoon tomato paste (concentrated purée)
125 ml (4 fl oz/½ cup) chicken stock
1 teaspoon smoked paprika
10 g (¼ oz/¼ cup) finely chopped flat-leaf
    (Italian) parsley
lemon wedges, to serve

Preheat the oven to 180°C (350°F). Pour half the oil into a large baking dish, add the potatoes, then transfer to the oven and cook for 30 minutes. The potatoes will still be firm, but will continue cooking with the fish.

Meanwhile, heat the remaining oil in a large frying pan over high heat. Season the fish cutlets with sea salt and freshly ground black pepper. Add the fish to the pan and cook for 3 minutes on each side, or until golden.

Lay the fish on the potatoes in the baking dish. Randomly place the chorizo, onion and olives over the fish.

Combine the tomato paste and stock in a small bowl or jug and pour over the fish. Sprinkle over the paprika. Cover with foil, ensuring the edges are sealed; this really helps to cook everything. Return the dish to the oven and cook for 20 minutes, or until the fish is cooked through.

Scatter the parsley over the top and serve with lemon wedges to squeeze over the fish and chorizo—this will really lift the flavours. Serve with crusty bread, rice or salad.

NEXT TIME *The baked mackerel would be great with couscous. When I make couscous, I don't follow the packet instructions exactly. The directions recommend using boiling water, but I find this can overcook the couscous grains, causing them to clump together, rendering the grains impossible to separate. My preferred method is to simply combine 190 g (6¾ oz/1 cup) couscous with 250 ml (9 fl oz/1 cup) warm tap water in a bowl. Stir quickly with a fork, then cover and set aside for 10 minutes. Stir again and cover for another 5 minutes. Fluff up the grains with a fork and season to taste before serving.*

This recipe takes its inspiration from a meal I once ate at a French bistro. The beef cheeks were meltingly tender and the sauce was so delicious that I wanted to pick up the plate and drink what I hadn't already mopped up with my French fries. This recipe combines the best of both worlds: a hearty beef stew served with golden, crisp fries tumbled on top. Perfect for a chilly day.

beef cheek stew
with french fries

6 beef cheeks, each cut in half
75 g (2½ oz/½ cup) plain (all-purpose) flour
60 ml (2 fl oz/¼ cup) olive oil
50 g (1¾ oz) butter
2 onions, finely chopped
1 carrot, coarsely grated
2 celery stalks, coarsely grated
2 garlic cloves, finely chopped
1 bay leaf
1 teaspoon ground star anise
3 tablespoons tomato paste (concentrated purée)
750 ml (26 fl oz/3 cups) red wine
250 ml (9 fl oz/1 cup) chicken stock

FRENCH FRIES
6 large roasting potatoes, such as russet (idaho), kennebec
    or coliban, cut into 5 mm (¼ inch) thick chips
2 litres (70 fl oz/8 cups) vegetable oil

Preheat the oven to 150°C (300°F). Put the beef cheeks in a colander with the flour and season well with sea salt and freshly ground black pepper. Toss the beef around to coat in the flour, shaking off the excess.

Heat the oil and butter in a heavy-based frying pan over medium heat. When the butter has melted and starts to sizzle, add half the beef cheeks and cook for 8–10 minutes, until well browned all over. Remove to a baking dish or casserole dish and repeat with the remaining beef.

Add the onions, carrot, celery, garlic, bay leaf and star anise to the pan and stir-fry for 8–10 minutes, until the vegetables are soft and golden. Add the tomato paste, then pour in the wine and stock, scraping the bottom of the pan to remove any bits that are stuck.

Pour the mixture over the beef cheeks. Cover the dish with foil or a tight-fitting lid and cook in the oven for 4 hours, or until the beef is fork tender. Remove from the oven and set aside, covered, to keep warm while you cook the fries.

To make the French fries, put the sliced potatoes and oil in a large saucepan over high heat. When the oil heats up and starts to sizzle, cook the potatoes for 25–30 minutes. The potatoes will cook in the centre first, but as the oil starts to bubble and boil, the potatoes will turn golden brown. Using kitchen tongs or a slotted spoon, remove the French fries from the oil and drain well on paper towel. Serve the beef cheeks with a stack of French fries piled on top.

NEXT TIME *Make a really rich and creamy mashed potato to serve with the beef cheeks instead of the fries. Peel and quarter 1 kg (2 lb 4 oz) mashing potatoes. Cook in boiling water until soft, then drain and return to the warm pan. Add 125 g (4½ oz) cubed butter, 125 ml (4 fl oz/½ cup) milk and sea salt, to taste. Use a potato masher to mash until combined, then use a large wooden spoon to whip the mixture until smooth and creamy.*

beef cheek stew with **french fries**   *page 182*

Asian pickles are packed full of heady spices and make a tasty addition to a cheese plate, and as a side to chicken schnitzel and curries. I like to whiz up a spicy marinade in the food processor with some pickle, yoghurt and coriander (cilantro) to rub over the chicken before cooking it on top of a tray of sizzling onions in the oven. This is a great way to cater and an exciting take on the prosaic wrap.

lime and yoghurt chicken wraps

MARINADE
70 g (2½ oz/¼ cup) Indian lime pickle
2 large handfuls coriander (cilantro) leaves and stems, roughly chopped
390 g (13¾ oz/1½ cups) plain yoghurt
1 teaspoon salt

8 boneless, skinless chicken thigh fillets, cut into quarters
60 ml (2 fl oz/¼ cup) vegetable oil
3 white onions, thinly sliced
2 handfuls coriander (cilantro) leaves and stems, finely chopped
2 tomatoes, sliced
½ iceberg lettuce, thinly sliced
12 chapatis (or see flatbreads recipe, page 150)

To make the marinade, put the lime pickle, coriander, yoghurt and salt in a food processor. Process to make a smooth green paste and scrape into a bowl. Add the chicken and toss to coat in the spicy yoghurt. Cover and refrigerate for at least 3 hours or overnight (remove the chicken from the fridge 30 minutes before cooking).

Preheat the oven to 180°C (350°F). Pour the oil into a baking dish, then place in the oven for 10 minutes to heat the oil. Add the onions to the dish, stirring them around to separate the rings. Cook the onions for about 20 minutes, or until softened.

Lay the chicken pieces on top of the onions and scrape any marinade left in the bowl over the chicken. Return the dish to the oven and cook for 30–35 minutes, until the chicken is cooked through and golden. Scatter the coriander over the chicken and serve straight from the baking dish, with the tomatoes, lettuce and chapatis on the side.

NEXT TIME *Use the same weight of a sustainable fish such as flathead to replace the chicken. With their long finger-like shape, flathead fillets are perfect for a wrap, sandwich or roll. But the fish will need less cooking time: only 15–20 minutes, until cooked through.*

We all like to cheat when cooking, especially when we have to cook something for a party or small gathering. I am all for the convenience of using good-quality sauces and curry pastes from the supermarket to make life a little easier. However, to lift the flavours and make your own stamp on the recipe, it's important to use some fresh ingredients too, such as onions, garlic, ginger, vine-ripened or truss tomatoes, herbs and your favourite spices. This recipe can easily be doubled to feed a larger group.

baked green masala fish

2 teaspoons ready-made green
    masala paste
2 garlic cloves, finely chopped
1 tablespoon grated fresh ginger
1 teaspoon fennel seeds
1 teaspoon ground cumin
2 red onions, thinly sliced
600 g (1 lb 5 oz) firm white fish
    fillets, such as blue eye, cut into
    150 g (5½ oz) pieces

2 tablespoons vegetable oil
8 small truss tomatoes
1 handful coriander (cilantro)
    leaves, roughly chopped
260 g (9¼ oz/1 cup) plain yoghurt
1 lemon, cut into wedges
Indian naan bread, to serve

Combine the masala paste, garlic, ginger, fennel seeds, cumin, onions and 3 tablespoons water in a large bowl. Add the fish pieces and gently toss to coat in the paste. Set aside for 30 minutes.

Preheat the oven to 180°C (350°F). Line a baking dish with baking paper. Drizzle the oil into the dish, then put the dish in the oven for 10 minutes, to heat up and kick-start the cooking process.

Tumble the marinated fish and onion marinade into the hot dish. Use kitchen tongs to move the fish pieces around so they are not overlapping. Randomly put the tomatoes in between the pieces of fish. Cook in the oven for 30 minutes, or until the fish is tender, the onions and tomatoes are soft and the spices are aromatic.

Scatter the coriander over the fish. Place the baking dish on the table and serve with the yoghurt, lemon wedges and bread on the side.

NEXT TIME *Replace the fish with large, raw prawns (shrimp), peeled and deveined. The cooking time for prawns is less than for the fish: 15-20 minutes. Serve with steamed rice instead of the bread.*

sweet as, bro

Some say there is always room for dessert. Others say that we have a separate stomach just to cater for it. And then there are others who believe that a sweet dish to finish a meal will elate even the most over-fed, sluggish individual into fits of giggles and chatty conversation. This is known as the post-dinner sugar high. And I like it.

Have you ever experienced that feeling after a big meal when you crave something sweet? It's almost murderous. Well, there is something here for just about every sweet tooth. Are you a chocolate or a lemon person? Do you prefer cake or pudding? Eggy and rich or light and fruity? Hot or cold?

Many of these desserts can be prepared a day in advance. But because we aren't always so well organised, some of these recipes take no time at all.

Sweet as.

No guessing where this pudding originates. This traditional Egyptian dessert is usually made with cooked puff pastry, but I couldn't resist using croissants. It's best to use croissants that are a day or two old.

pharaoh's pudding

4 large croissants, about 250 g (9 oz) total weight
50 g (1¾ oz/½ cup) flaked almonds
40 g (1½ oz/¼ cup) pine nuts
35 g (1¼ oz/¼ cup) pistachio nuts
10–12 dried pitted dates, chopped
20 g (¾ oz/¼ cup) shredded coconut

500 ml (17 fl oz/2 cups) full-cream (whole) milk
2 eggs
1 teaspoon natural vanilla extract
110 g (3¾ oz/½ cup) sugar
125 ml (4 fl oz/½ cup) whipping cream
2 tablespoons icing (confectioners') sugar

Preheat the oven to 180°C (350°F). Lightly grease a 3 litre (105 fl oz/12 cup capacity) baking dish with butter. Tear the croissants into large bite-sized pieces and put half of the croissant pieces into the dish.

Combine the almonds, pine nuts, pistachios, dates and coconut in a bowl. Combine the milk, eggs and vanilla in another bowl.

Sprinkle half the nut mixture over the croissants, sprinkle half the sugar over the top, then pour over half the milk mixture. Repeat, adding another layer of croissants, the remaining nut mixture and sugar. Pour the remaining milk mixture over the top.

Beat the cream until thickened, taking care not to overbeat the cream or it will be grainy. Spoon the cream over the pudding, then gently spread to evenly cover the top. Sift over the icing sugar. Transfer to the oven and bake for 30–35 minutes, until golden. Serve hot.

Use chocolate croissants or 4 large slices of brioche instead of the plain croissants.

Kids will love this because it has a bit of magic. Hot liquid is poured over a batter and this looks like a real mess until it's put in the oven. Somehow the hot liquid makes its way to the bottom of the dish to make a delicious sauce that sits underneath a light, golden sponge.

butterscotch pudding

SAUCE
175 g (6 oz/^{1}/$_2$ cup) golden syrup
   or treacle
100 g (3^1/$_2$ oz/^{1}/$_2$ cup, lightly
   packed) light brown sugar

PUDDING
300 g (10^1/$_2$ oz/2 cups) plain
   (all-purpose) flour
1 tablespoon baking powder
220 g (7^3/$_4$ oz/1 cup) caster
   (superfine) sugar
100 g (3^1/$_2$ oz) unsalted butter,
   melted
500 ml (17 fl oz/2 cups) milk
2 eggs, lightly whisked
2 teaspoons natural vanilla extract

Preheat the oven to 180°C (350°F). Lightly grease a 1.5–2 litre (52–70 fl oz/ 6–8 cup capacity) baking dish with butter.

To make the sauce, combine the golden syrup, brown sugar and 375 ml (13 fl oz/1½ cups) water in a small saucepan. Set aside.

To make the pudding, combine the flour, baking powder and caster sugar in a bowl. Whisk in the melted butter, milk, eggs and vanilla until well combined. Pour into the prepared baking dish.

Cook the golden syrup mixture over high heat. When the mixture comes to the boil, carefully and slowly pour it over the pudding in the baking dish. Bake in the oven for 35–40 minutes, until the top of the pudding is golden and cooked through, and the butterscotch sauce has formed in the bottom of the dish. Serve hot with thick cream or ice cream.

NEXT TIME *Thinly slice a banana and lay it on the bottom of the baking dish. Sprinkle a handful of chocolate chips over the banana, then pour the pudding mixture into the dish, as per the recipe above.*

You could think of the traditional trifle, with its delicate layers of berries, jelly, cake and whipped cream, as being feminine, while I see this contemporary version as somewhat more masculine. The caramel here is really the cheat's way of making *dulce de leche*, the South American sweeter than sweet sauce. Gently heating the condensed milk and molasses for a short time results in a thick and rich caramel.

caramel and banana trifle

CARAMEL
2 x 395 g (14 oz) tins sweetened condensed milk
80 ml (2½ fl oz/⅓ cup) molasses

COCONUT CUSTARD
80 g (2¾ oz) instant custard powder or instant
   vanilla pudding powder
750 ml (26 fl oz/3 cups) milk
3 tablespoons caster (superfine) sugar
½ teaspoon coconut essence or flavouring
35 g (1¼ oz/½ cup) shredded coconut (use
   'moist shredded coconut' if available)

VANILLA CREAM
375 ml (13 fl oz/1½ cups) whipping cream
2 teaspoons vanilla essence
30 g (1 oz/¼ cup) icing (confectioners') sugar

24 ready-made Anzac biscuits (cookies) or other
   oat-based biscuits
200 ml (7 fl oz) dark rum
2 large bananas
35 g (1¼ oz/½ cup) shredded coconut, toasted

To make the caramel, combine the condensed milk and molasses in a small saucepan and stir over medium heat for 2–3 minutes, until thick and caramel in colour. Remove from the heat and leave at room temperature.

To make the coconut custard, combine the custard powder, milk and sugar in a small saucepan over medium heat. Cook, whisking constantly, until the mixture thickens. Remove from the heat and allow to cool for 10 minutes. Stir in the coconut essence and coconut and refrigerate.

To make the vanilla cream, beat the cream, vanilla and icing sugar until the cream is thick. Refrigerate until needed.

Put the biscuits in the bottom of a large glass bowl or dish, breaking them up a little so they cover the base of the bowl. Pour the rum evenly over the biscuits.

Spoon the caramel over the biscuit layer, then slice one banana and arrange the slices on the caramel. Spoon the coconut custard over the bananas. Slice the remaining banana and place on the custard. Top with the vanilla cream and spread to smooth.

Refrigerate for up to 6 hours before serving. The trifle can be left in the fridge overnight, but this does affect the texture a little. Just before you are ready to serve, scatter the toasted coconut over the top.

 Spoon any leftovers into a loaf (bar) pan and freeze. Cut into slices and serve.

caramel and **banana trifle** *page 196*

custard filo pie with **floral syrup**   *page 200*

Custards in Middle Eastern and Mediterranean cookery are a relatively fuss-free affair. A low and gentle heat is all that is needed to warm milk and, occasionally, cream. Some sugar and aromatics are added to the milk, as well as eggs and a thickener such as rice flour or fine semolina. The cooled custard is then shrouded in fine filo pastry and baked until golden. But the goodness doesn't stop there. The whole lot is then drowned in a sweet orange blossom syrup and will last for several days in the fridge.

custard filo pie
with floral syrup

1.5 litres (52 fl oz/6 cups) milk
180 g (6½ oz/1 cup) fine semolina
165 g (5¾ oz/¾ cup) caster (superfine) sugar
1 teaspoon natural vanilla extract
3 eggs, lightly whisked
9 sheets filo pastry
80 g (2¾ oz) unsalted butter, melted

SYRUP
165 g (5¾ oz/¾ cup) caster (superfine) sugar
1 teaspoon rosewater
1 teaspoon orange blossom water

Combine the milk, semolina, sugar and vanilla in a saucepan and stir over low heat for about 10 minutes, or until the mixture thickens slightly and looks like a thin custard. Remove from the heat and set aside for 10 minutes.

Use a whisk to slowly beat the eggs into the cooled custard mixture. Continue whisking until all the egg has been added and the custard is smooth. Set aside.

Preheat the oven to 160°C (320°F). Brush a 20 cm (8 inch) square deep-sided baking dish or cake tin with butter.

Lay a sheet of filo pastry on a clean work surface and lightly brush all over with a little melted butter. Lay another sheet of filo on top and brush with butter. Repeat with another sheet of filo and butter. Lay this stack of filo into the prepared baking dish, gently pressing the filo into the corners and sides of the dish, and allowing the excess filo to overhang the sides.

Repeat the layering and buttering with three more sheets of filo. Lay this stack of filo into the dish, placing it in the opposite direction on top of the first stack. Allow the excess filo to overhang the sides. Pour the custard over the filo, spreading it out to the edges.

Brush the remaining three sheets of filo with butter, as previously, then fold this stack in half. Lay the filo on top of the custard. Brush the top of the filo with butter and neatly fold over all the overhanging filo to enclose the custard. Brush the top of the pie with any remaining butter. Transfer to the oven and bake for 1 hour, or until the pastry is golden. Remove and set aside.

To make the syrup, combine the sugar and 185 ml (6 fl oz/¾ cup) water in a small saucepan. Cook over medium heat, stirring occasionally, for about 10 minutes, or until syrupy. Stir in the rosewater and orange blossom water.

Place a large serving plate over the filo pie and then turn the pie out onto the plate. Pour the syrup over the pie and let it sit at room temperature for at least 2 hours, or refrigerate. Cut into slices and serve.

 Add a cupful of sultanas (golden raisins) to the custard mixture before putting the remaining three layers of filo on top.

With its tangy, tropical flavour, passionfruit is great in baking and desserts, and seems a natural fit in this version of the ever-popular lemon delicious. Lemon delicious seems to be the unique name given to a self-saucing pudding in Australia and New Zealand. Elsewhere, it is generally referred to as a lemon pudding.

passionfruit delish

3 eggs, separated
110 g (3¾ oz/½ cup) caster
   (superfine) sugar
60 ml (2 fl oz/¼ cup) passionfruit
   pulp and seeds

30 g (1 oz) unsalted butter, melted
250 ml (9 fl oz/1 cup) milk
35 g (1¼ oz/¼ cup) self-raising
   flour
2 tablespoons lemon juice

Preheat the oven to 180°C (350°F). Lightly grease a 1.5–2 litre (52–70 fl oz/ 6–8 cup capacity) baking dish with butter.

Beat the egg yolks and sugar using electric beaters until pale and creamy. Beat in the passionfruit pulp until combined, then beat in the melted butter, milk and flour until well combined. Add the lemon juice and stir to combine.

In a separate bowl, beat the egg whites until firm peaks form. Fold the egg whites, in two batches, into the pudding mixture.

Pour into the prepared dish and cook in the oven for 50–55 minutes, until risen and golden brown. Serve hot with cream.

 NEXT TIME *For an equally citrusy and zesty flavour, use lime juice instead of lemon juice, or a mixture of both.*

Steamed puddings are a great treat, but they are often overlooked. I think this is because they are thought of as old fashioned, and they are. But this isn't a bad thing. They are a comforting and humble pudding, perfect for those chilly winter nights.

orange and coconut steamed pudding

2 tablespoons orange marmalade
100 g (3½ oz) unsalted butter,
    at room temperature
110 g (3¾ oz/½ cup) caster
    (superfine) sugar
1 egg, lightly whisked
1 tablespoon finely grated orange
    zest

60 ml (2 fl oz/¼ cup) freshly
    squeezed orange juice
225 g (8 oz/1½ cups) self-raising
    flour
1 tablespoon desiccated (finely
    shredded) coconut

Lightly grease a 1 litre (35 fl oz/4 cup capacity) pudding basin (mould) with butter and place a small square of baking paper on the base. Spoon the marmalade into the basin.

Beat the butter and sugar using electric beaters for 4–5 minutes, until pale and creamy. Slowly beat in the egg, then stir in the orange zest, juice, flour and coconut to make a smooth batter.

Scrape the mixture into the pudding basin. Cover with the lid and put into a large saucepan. Pour enough boiling water into the saucepan to come about halfway up the side of the basin. Cover the saucepan and steam the pudding for 1½ hours over medium heat, topping up with water as needed to maintain a constant level.

Remove the pudding basin from the saucepan. Leave the lid on and allow to cool for 15 minutes, then remove the lid and invert the pudding onto a serving plate. Serve with cream or ice cream.

 Substitute the marmalade for any other marmalade or jam. Try lime marmalade or strawberry jam.

Funny stuff this rhubarb. It's in season only for a short time and it seems to me that many of us just don't know what to do with it. Rhubarb is technically a vegetable, but I can't say that I've ever seen it used as one. Cooking or stewing it with sugar combats its tartness and turns it into a lovely hue of rose pink. Rhubarb is great in pies, cakes, muffins and crumbles.

spiced rhubarb cobbler

700 g (1 lb 9 oz) bunch rhubarb
110 g (3¾ oz/½ cup) caster
    (superfine) sugar
1 tablespoon finely grated
    lemon zest
3 cloves
1 cinnamon stick, crumbled

TOPPING
250 g (9 oz/1⅔ cups) self-raising
    flour
1 tablespoon caster (superfine)
    sugar
20 g (¾ oz) butter
1 teaspoon ground nutmeg
1 egg, lightly whisked
250 ml (9 fl oz/1 cup) milk

Preheat the oven to 180°C (350°F). Lightly grease a 1.5 litre (52 fl oz/6 cup capacity) baking dish with butter.

To prepare the rhubarb, cut off the green leaves and discard. Cut the stems into 2.5 cm (1 inch) lengths and then measure out 4 cups of the chopped rhubarb into a bowl.

Add the sugar, lemon zest, cloves and cinnamon to the rhubarb and stir to combine. Tumble the rhubarb mixture into the prepared dish. Bake in the oven for 15–20 minutes, until tender. Remove from the oven and leave to cool a little, then pick out the cloves and cinnamon and discard.

Meanwhile, to make the topping, combine the flour and sugar in a bowl. Add the butter and nutmeg and use your fingertips to rub the butter into the flour and sugar. Add the egg and milk and stir to make a thick scone-like batter. Dollop spoonfuls of the batter randomly over the rhubarb. Return the dish to the oven and bake for 25–30 minutes, until golden. Serve hot with ice cream or thick cream.

 No rhubarb? Use 4 cups of chopped cooking apples plus 1 cup of frozen blueberries.

Also known as shirt-sleeve pudding because of its resemblance to an arm in a long shirt, this pudding puts the 'old' in old school and was probably created in the days when necessity was the mother of invention. But to label this Depression Era food is to take away from it as being timeless comfort food. This is totally delicious served with warm custard.

jam roly poly

300 g (10½ oz/2 cups) plain (all-purpose) flour, plus 2 tablespoons extra
3 teaspoons baking powder
50 g (1¾ oz) unsalted butter
110 g (3¾ oz/½ cup) caster (superfine) sugar

125 ml (4 fl oz/½ cup) milk
250 g (9 oz/¾ cup) blackberry jam
2 tablespoons golden syrup or treacle
1 teaspoon ground cinnamon

Preheat the oven to 180°C (350°F). Put the flour, baking powder, butter and sugar in a food processor and pulse to combine. Add the milk and process for just a few seconds. Tip the mixture onto a floured work surface and roll into a rectangle about 20 x 30 cm (8 x 12 inches).

Combine the jam, golden syrup and cinnamon in a bowl. Spread the jam mixture over the dough. Working from the long side, roll the dough into a log.

Lay a clean kitchen cloth or muslin (cheesecloth), about 40 cm (16 inches) square, on the work surface and sprinkle with the extra flour. Lay the dough log on the cloth, placing it on the end nearest to you. Roll the cloth to enclose the log, tucking in the sides to secure.

Bring a large saucepan of water to the boil. The saucepan will need to measure at least 30 cm (12 inch) in diameter to fit the dough log. Lower the dough into the boiling water, then reduce the heat to medium and cover the pan. Cook for 1½ hours, topping up the water as needed, then remove the pudding from the water and allow to cool for 15 minutes.

Unwrap the cloth and cut the jam roly poly into 2 cm (¾ inch) thick slices. Serve hot with custard.

 Use another jam (fig is lovely) and add 60 g (2¼ oz/½ cup) chopped pecans or walnuts to the jam mixture.

These jaffa pots have the texture of a chocolate mousse, but they aren't quite so light—which is not to say these are heavy. A jaffa is a large, thick-skinned variety of orange. It also happens to be the name of an orange and chocolate lolly or candy, much loved in Australia and New Zealand.

jaffa pots

250 g (9 oz) dark chocolate, chopped
2 tablespoons sherry
20 g (¾ oz) unsalted butter
1 tablespoon finely grated orange zest

60 ml (2 fl oz/¼ cup) freshly squeezed orange juice
5 eggs, separated
almond bread, to serve

Put the chocolate, sherry and butter in a large heatproof bowl. Place the bowl over a small saucepan of simmering water, ensuring the base of the bowl isn't touching the water. Stir until the chocolate and butter have melted and all the ingredients are smoothly combined. Remove the bowl from the heat. Stir the orange zest and orange juice into the melted chocolate mixture.

Beat the egg yolks using an electric mixer until pale and well combined. Add to the chocolate mixture and stir until combined.

In a large, clean bowl, beat the egg whites until firm peaks form. Using a large spoon, fold the egg whites in two or three batches into the chocolate mixture.

Pour the chocolate mixture into eight small bowls or coffee cups and refrigerate for at least 3 hours, or until set firm. Serve with almond bread.

 For a more fragrant version, add 2 teaspoons orange blossom water or rosewater to the beaten egg yolks.

This crowd-pleasing pudding is made with brioche instead of bread. Some supermarkets now sell loaves of sliced brioche but if you struggle to find it, use stale white bread or even wholemeal bread. The rum and raisin flavours are quite grown up, so don't hold back: serve this with an espresso on the side.

rum and raisin brioche pudding

250 g (9 oz) brioche (about 1/2 loaf)
750 ml (26 fl oz/3 cups) milk
80 ml (2 1/2 fl oz/1/3 cup) Jamaican rum (or any dark rum)
50 g (1 3/4 oz) butter

1 teaspoon natural vanilla extract
45 g (1 1/2 oz/1/4 cup) raisins
75 g (2 1/2 oz/1/3 cup) sugar
3 eggs, lightly whisked

Preheat the oven to 180°C (350°F). Lightly grease a 2 litre (70 fl oz/8 cup capacity) baking dish with butter. Cut or tear the brioche slices into large bite-sized pieces, about 5 cm (2 inches) wide, then tip the bricohe into the dish, spreading the pieces out evenly.

Combine the milk, rum, butter, vanilla, raisins and sugar in a saucepan over low heat. Stir until the butter has melted and the mixture is aromatic. Remove from the heat and set aside to cool for 10 minutes. Slowly whisk the eggs into the milk mixture.

Pour the custard over the brioche and leave for 20–30 minutes, to allow the bread to soak up the custard—this will give the pudding a lighter, fluffier texture.

Bake for 30–45 minutes, until the custard is set but still a little wobbly and the edges of the brioche have browned. Serve warm or at room temperature with ice cream.

 Sprinkle 85 g (3 oz/1/2 cup) good-quality chocolate chips over the brioche in the baking dish, before pouring over the custard.

Next time you are at the supermarket or a large greengrocer, look down at the shelves at knee level. Here you will find all sorts of culinary oddities, including morello cherries. They are soft, sweet and ready to go, any time of the year.

apple and cherry pie

330 g (11½ oz/1½ cups) caster (superfine) sugar
1 tablespoon ground cinnamon
4 small granny smith apples, peeled and roughly chopped
200 g (7 oz/1 cup) pitted morello cherries

3 eggs
375 ml (13 fl oz/1½ cups) vegetable oil
1 teaspoon natural vanilla extract
225 g (8 oz/1½ cups) plain (all-purpose) flour
½ teaspoon baking powder

Preheat the oven to 180°C (350°F). Lightly grease a 1.5 litre (52 fl oz/6 cup capacity) round baking dish or deep pie tin.

Combine the sugar and cinnamon in a small bowl. Put the apples and cherries in a bowl with 2 tablespoons of the cinnamon sugar. Toss the fruit around to coat in the sugar, then tumble into the dish.

Beat the eggs and oil until light and fluffy. Add the vanilla and stir until combined, then add the flour, baking powder and remaining cinnamon sugar and stir until smooth. Pour the batter over the fruit. Bake in the oven for 50–60 minutes, or until risen and aromatic. Allow to cool a little before serving with cream or ice cream.

NEXT TIME *Use chopped pears instead of apples and add 1 teaspoon ground cardamom to the cinnamon and sugar mixture for a really fragrant, spiced pie.*

S
W
E
E
T

A
S,

B
R
O

Crumbles are the best thing to make in autumn and winter. Autumnal fruits (such as apples and pears) and frozen summer berries make a perfect combination. The pears stay firm while the berry juices bleed into the crumble, providing tartness and colour.

pear and blackberry cornflake crumble

CORNFLAKE CRUMBLE
150 g (5½ oz) unsalted butter, grated
60 g (2¼ oz/2 cups) cornflakes
225 g (8 oz/1½ cups) plain (all-purpose) flour
220 g (7¾ oz/1 cup) sugar

200 g (7 oz) frozen blackberries
2 firm brown pears, chopped into 2 cm (¾ inch) pieces
3 tablespoons sugar
1 tablespoon cornflour (cornstarch)
2 teaspoons lemon juice
1 teaspoon orange blossom water (optional)

Preheat the oven to 180°C (350°F). Lightly grease a 1–1.5 litre (35–52 fl oz/ 4–6 cup capacity) baking dish with butter.

To make the cornflake crumble, put all the crumble ingredients in a bowl and use your fingertips to combine. Refrigerate until needed.

Put the blackberries and pears in a bowl. Sprinkle with the sugar and cornflour and toss the fruit to evenly combine. Add the lemon juice and orange blossom water, if using, and gently stir to combine.

Tumble the fruit mixture into the prepared dish. Sprinkle the crumble mixture evenly over the fruit. Bake in the oven for 25–30 minutes, until the crumble is golden. Serve with ice cream or cream.

 Substitute the pears for apples and the blueberries for fresh or frozen raspberries, strawberries or a forest berry mix.

There are a few stories going around about how this Spanish dish got its unusual name. One story goes along the lines that pork was so scarce and considered a luxury food, so this dessert was whipped up to mimic the look of a slow-cooked piece of pork belly. Other stories suggest that the bacon is really just a metaphor for something delicious—which this is.

heaven's bacon

220 g (7¾ oz/1 cup) sugar
600 ml (21 fl oz) milk
395 g (14 oz) tin sweetened
    condensed milk

12 eggs
1 teaspoon natural vanilla extract

Preheat the oven to 180°C (350°F). Put the sugar and 125 ml (4 fl oz/½ cup) water in a saucepan and cook over medium heat. Swirl and tilt the pan to move the melted sugar syrup around so it cooks evenly. Continue to cook until all the sugar has dissolved and turns a straw colour.

Pour the caramel into a 20 cm (8 inch) square baking dish or cake tin. Tilt the dish so the toffee covers the entire base. Set aside.

Beat the milk, condensed milk, eggs and vanilla for 2–3 minutes using an electric mixer, until well combined. Pour the custard through a fine sieve, directly into the baking dish. Sit the dish in a large baking tin. Pour enough boiling water into the tin to come about halfway up the sides of the baking dish. Transfer to the oven and cook for 45 minutes. Remove and set aside to cool a little, then refrigerate to cool completely.

When you are ready to serve, run a small, sharp knife around the edge of the pudding. Place a large plate on top, then quickly flip the plate over, so the pudding tips out of the dish. Pour any extra caramel over the top, then cut into rectangles to serve.

NEXT TIME *Whip 250 ml (9 fl oz/1 cup) cream with 1 tablespoon rosewater, 1 teaspoon natural vanilla extract and 3 tablespoons icing (confectioners') sugar until thick. Serve dollops of cream over the pudding.*

Mix-and-bake, foolproof and delicious. These are some of the words to describe this cake, which takes very little time to prepare and will keep for several days.

chocolate, almond and date cake

300 g (10½ oz) dark chocolate, chopped
395 g (14 oz) tin sweetened condensed milk
2 tablespoons molasses
300 g (10½ oz/2 cups) whole almonds
125 g (4½ oz/¾ cup) chopped dates
5 eggs

CHOCOLATE GANACHE
125 ml (4 fl oz/½ cup) whipping cream,
    at room temperature
200 g (7 oz) dark chocolate, chopped

Preheat the oven to 180°C (350°F). Assemble a 24 cm (9½ inch) spring-form cake tin. Tear off two sheets of baking paper to a size that will easily fit into the tin, leaving some excess paper to overhang the side. Rinse the paper in cold water, then wring out the excess water—the paper will resemble crinkly fabric. Use the paper to line the cake tin.

Put the chocolate in a heatproof bowl. Place the bowl over a small saucepan of simmering water, ensuring the base of the bowl isn't touching the water. Use a rubber spatula or wooden spoon to stir the chocolate until it starts to melt. Stir in the condensed milk and molasses until combined. Remove from the heat.

Put the almonds in a food processor and process until finely chopped. Add the chopped dates and process again until the almonds and dates are well combined and finely chopped. Add the chocolate mixture to the almonds and dates. The mixture will seem impossibly thick at first, but start to add the eggs, one at a time, and process for a few seconds to make a thick, nutty batter. Scrape the mixture into the prepared tin and bake for 40 minutes, or until slightly risen. Leave in the tin to cool a little.

To make the chocolate ganache, put the cream in a heatproof bowl and place the bowl over a small saucepan of simmering water. Add the chocolate and stir until smooth and silky.

Leaving the cake in the tin, pour the ganache over the cake. Allow the cake to cool completely. The cake can be refrigerated for a couple of days. Run a warmed, small knife around the edge of the tin and remove the cake. Serve at room temperature or chilled from the fridge.

NEXT TIME *There are so many variations you could use for this cake. I think almonds work best here, but walnuts could be used instead. Add prunes instead of dates. You could also add some ground cinnamon or a teaspoon of rosewater or orange blossom water.*

chocolate, almond and date cake *page 218*

When I was looking through some of my mum's old recipes, I found a half-written recipe for this cake. She used tinned mango but I'd much prefer to use fresh. This cake is really halfway between an indulgent afternoon tea cake and a rich, fruity Christmas cake.

tropical fruit cake

1 large, ripe mango
50 g (1¾ oz) unsalted butter
500 g (1 lb 2 oz) mixed dried fruit
100 g (3½ oz/½ cup, lightly packed) light brown sugar
1½ teaspoons bicarbonate of soda (baking soda)
35 g (1¼ oz/½ cup) shredded coconut

225 g (8 oz/1½ cups) plain (all-purpose) flour
1 teaspoon baking powder
450 g (1 lb) tin crushed pineapple
2 eggs, lightly whisked
1 teaspoon natural vanilla extract
2 tablespoons golden syrup or treacle

Preheat the oven to 180°C (350°F). Line the base of a 23 cm (9 inch) spring-form cake tin with baking paper and lightly grease the base and side with butter or vegetable oil.

Peel the mango and roughly chop the flesh into 1–2 cm (½–¾ inch) pieces. Put the mango in a small saucepan with the butter, dried fruit, brown sugar, bicarbonate of soda and 125 ml (4 fl oz/½ cup) water. Place the pan over high heat and stir to combine. As soon as the mixture boils, remove the pan from the heat and set aside.

Combine the coconut, flour and baking powder in a bowl. Add the mango mixture and crushed pineapple, then stir in the eggs and vanilla until well combined. Pour the mixture into the prepared tin. Bake for 40–45 minutes, until the cake has risen to a golden top. Remove the cake from the oven and brush the top with golden syrup. Set aside to cool for 10 minutes before removing from the tin.

NEXT TIME *Decorate the top of the cake with 80 g (2¾ oz/½ cup) blanched whole almonds before baking, or pour 250 ml (9 fl oz/1 cup) dark rum over the cake while it is still hot. Serve warm with vanilla or coconut ice cream.*

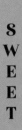

index

Published in 2017 by Murdoch Books, an imprint of Allen & Unwin

Murdoch Books Australia
83 Alexander Street
Crows Nest NSW 2065
Phone: +61 (0) 2 8425 0100
Fax: +61 (0) 2 9906 2218
murdochbooks.com.au
info@murdochbooks.com.au

Murdoch Books UK
Ormond House
26–27 Boswell Street
London WC1N 3JZ
Phone: +44 (0) 20 8785 5995
murdochbooks.co.uk
info@murdochbooks.co.uk

For Corporate Orders & Custom Publishing,
contact our Business Development Team at
salesenquiries@murdochbooks.com.au.

Publisher: Diana Hill
Editorial Manager: Emma Hutchinson
Design Manager: Madeleine Kane
Project Editor: Kim Rowney
Designer: Hugh Ford
Photographer: Steve Brown
Stylist: Matt Page
Home Economist: Grace Campbell
Production Manager: Rachel Walsh

A cataloguing-in-publication entry is available
from the catalogue of the National Library of Australia
at nla.gov.au.

ISBN 978 1 74336 861 9 Australia
ISBN 978 1 74336 862 6 UK

A catalogue record for this book is available from the
British Library.

Colour reproduction by Splitting Image Colour Studio
Pty Ltd, Clayton, Victoria
Printed by 1010 Printing International Limited, China

IMPORTANT: Those who might
be at risk from the effects of
salmonella poisoning (the elderly,
pregnant women, young children
and those suffering from immune
deficiency diseases) should consult
their doctor with any concerns
about eating raw eggs.

OVEN GUIDE: You may find
cooking times vary depending
on the oven you are using. For
fan-forced ovens, as a general
rule, set the oven temperature to
20°C (70°F) lower than indicated
in the recipe.

MEASURES GUIDE:
We have used 20 ml (4 teaspoon)
tablespoon measures. If you are
using a 15 ml (3 teaspoon)
tablespoon add an extra
teaspoon of the ingredient for
each tablespoon specified.